The *re* in refuge

ALSO BY ADRIANNE KALFOPOULOU

Poetry
Wild Greens
Passion Maps
A History of Too Much

Prose
Ruin, essays in exilic living
On the Gaze: Dubai and its New Cosmopolitanisms

Translations
Ξένη, Ξένο, Ξενιτιά with Katerina Iliopoulou

The *re* in refuge

essays

ADRIANNE KALFOPOULOU

Red Hen Press | *Pasadena, CA*

Book design by Mark E. Cull

Library of Congress Cataloging-in-Publication Data

Names: Kalfopoulou, Adrianne, author.
Title: The re in refuge: essays / Adrianne Kalfopoulou.
Description: First edition. | Pasadena, CA: Red Hen Press, 2025. |
  Includes bibliographical references.
Identifiers: LCCN 2024042069 (print) | LCCN 2024042070 (ebook) | ISBN
  9781636282763 (paperback) | ISBN 9781636282770 (ebook)
Subjects: LCSH: Refuge (Humanitarian assistance)—Social aspects. | Refuge
  (Humanitarian assistance)—Political aspects. | Refugees—Social
  conditions. | Refugees—Public opinion. | LCGFT: Essays.
Classification: LCC HV640 .K35 2025 (print) | LCC HV640 (ebook) | DDC
  362.87—dc23/eng/20241108
LC record available at https://lccn.loc.gov/2024042069
LC ebook record available at https://lccn.loc.gov/2024042070

The National Endowment for the Arts, the Los Angeles County Arts Commission, the Ah-
manson Foundation, the Dwight Stuart Youth Fund, the Max Factor Family Foundation, the
Pasadena Tournament of Roses Foundation, the Pasadena Arts & Culture Commission and
the City of Pasadena Cultural Affairs Division, the City of Los Angeles Department of Cultural Affairs, the Audrey & Sydney Irmas Charitable Foundation, the Meta & George Rosenberg
Foundation, the Albert and Elaine Borchard Foundation, the Adams Family Foundation, Amazon Literary Partnership, the Sam Francis Foundation, and the Mara W. Breech Foundation
partially support Red Hen Press.

   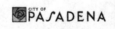 

First Edition
Published by Red Hen Press
www.redhen.org

ACKNOWLEDGEMENTS

My sincere thanks to these journals, and their editors, for giving these essays and poems a home:

"*In shā' Allāh,*" *Eryon, Greek/American & Diaspora Arts and Letters*; "~~Left behind~~ for a square of space," *Inverted Syntax*; "Transitional Object, a grammar for letting go," *Juked*; "Water," *Partisan Hotel*; "The Parts Don't Add Up," *Slag Glass City*; "The Journey Where," "The Wig & The Scream," *Superstition Review*; "The Unhoused," *Superstition Review* blog post; "*Psyhi mou,*" *The Common*.

Deep gratitude, *shukran, tashakor, efcharistó, merci,* and thank you to all in these pages, you've been my muse, and amplified my world ♥! Thanks to Michel Pharand and Ashlyn Petro for invaluable edits, and careful attention to this work.

Kate and Mark, and everyone in the Red Hen coop, such gratitude and appreciation for all you do, and for your ongoing faith in my work.

All photographs are my own, except for the image on p. 90 by Maedeh Mohibi, used with permission.

for Eleni Bastéa, 1958–2020

Lying on a floor
In California
Talking on the phone with me, I see the light
The floor, you
Covered in sun

CONTENTS

The *re* in refuge

Life is created by events, but it is only when we are able to interpret them . . . and lend them meaning that they are transformed into experience.
—Olga Tokarczuk, "The Tender Narrator"

Does every exile want to run backward after a time?
—Dina Nayeri, *The Ungrateful Refugee*

In shā' Allāh

He will go with a new name, passport, discover a newly hired parent at the port.
Europe's borders closed; illegal journeys will now begin anew at the port.

I'm called by my passport name, buy food, cook with groceries I can bring home.
Vitamins and toothpaste, I say to the boy who asks me for shoes at the port.

An Afghan girl grabs my hand, points to her rotting teeth, repeats, *me! me! me!*
Her brother has soccer cards, thirty euros, dreams he's a goalie & waits at the port.

If you're Syrian you'll have less trouble getting papers, otherwise sell jewelry,
bribe your way, bargain a stolen cell phone, be sure not to get stuck at the port.

I wake in the middle of the night thinking I forgot to say, *Bring water with you.*
Ali says, *thank you*, his English polite, his manners promise safe passage at the port.

Boats appear, many disappear, sunk with people who sold everything for some luck.
Smugglers are on the lookout, they know opportunity, and smell profit at the port.

God be with you, Judi says, holding her hand to her heart. *In shā' Allāh,* Azize says.
We pray *Allāh* is welcoming, a father who won't abandon his children at the port.

OF EVENT

What came to words out of embodied events was often born of a failure to match that sense of immersion in language. I think of the materiality of occasions, as in the 2015 European refugee crisis, the caregivers in the global COVID-19 pandemic, those pulling loved ones out from under the rubble in Gaza: such occasions equal any impulse of art or, for me, preface it.

The poet Valzhyna Mort, who has been tweeting on the torture and incarceration of the Belarusian people by Alexander Lukashensko's regime, tweeted this sentence by Flaubert one morning: "The one way of tolerating existence is to lose oneself in literature as in a perpetual orgy." Waving red and white flowers on the streets of Minsk to protest Lukashensko's rigged August 2022 election results, those enacting their solidarity become a poetry of their own; Mort sends "flowers and cake" to her Belarus friends when they are released from prison.

Eleni Bastéa and I met in October 2017 when she gave the Eleftherios Venizelos Chair lecture at the American College of Greece. The title of her talk was "The Memory of Home Across the Aegean: Greek & Turkish Reflections on Loss." I asked a question during the Q&A which had to do with Orhan Pamuk's *Istanbul*, and how Eleni spoke of Thessaloniki, her birth city, and her background as the daughter of a family in the forced population exchange between Turkey and Greece. We continued conversations over emails, and Eleni invited me to give a lecture at the International Studies Institute at the University of New Mexico where she was the Regents Professor of Architecture. Eleni was a Stanford Humanities Center fellow writing a book titled *Geographies of Loss* when she lost her life to cancer; it was another confluence of events.

Displacement makes of the "I"—or any first-person positioning—a "You." It teaches you to pay attention to what the I might not see. In Rana Kazkaz's fourteen-minute film short, *Mare Nostrum*, a father throws his twelve-year-old daughter into the sea. Neither of them knows how to swim. The film is without dialogue. We watch the unfolding of events. My students assumed the refugee father was a bad person because he throws his daughter—who thinks they are playing a game—into a sea that will either save or kill them. The daughter is then mean to the father who, to her mind, betrayed her trust. In the only voice we hear (that of a news commentator) at the end of the film, the daughter is a statistic, one of the Syrians in an overturned dinghy in the Aegean to have survived. We assume the father didn't, though he had taught her to swim.

I

THE JOURNEY WHERE

Continent, city, country, society:
the choice is never wide and never free.
　　　　　　　—Elizabeth Bishop, "Questions of Travel"

Wine

I woke up with the word "lettuce" in my mind and remembered my daughter eating a head of it for her dinner on a plate in the living room. There was also the word "ferociously" in the dream. I was eating ferociously. As in travel, everything felt not quite where it ought to be. My love said to me, "Traveling alone you find yourself in an existentialist space. But with someone, you're more enclosed," in the "us," I wanted to say, that domesticates the journey. A sense of "us" gives reference, we're aware of the other listening. This was what terrified me most. No one seemed to be listening as I traveled. Despite the frequency of nouns like "connections" and adjectives like "shared" in my movement through airport terminals and security checkpoints where ads and PA announcements tried to reassure me of my future and my safety, I felt disconnected from "us." A script was at work that made listening difficult, so I took notes and recorded words. Some, like the lettuce in my dream, added color. I was also reading Susan Stewart's *The Poet's Freedom*, *A Notebook on Making*. She had this to say: "Freedom lies thereby in giving one's self one's own law out of one's own essence." I understood essence to mean a vitality that contains its own laws. A word like "organic," for example, suggests that volition is innate to the essence of living.

"Your DNA Is Your Data," an HSBC ad notes at Heathrow. According to HSBC, in the "emerging future," essence will equal information, "Nature and Technology will work as one"—will this include volition, the choice of "*giving* one's self"? Stewart's sense of "one's own law" will then become a quantifiable essence according to HSBC—I was traveling across the Atlantic to my love as well as for work but couldn't always keep up with the shifting time zones, let alone the changing laws of security. I was traveling to keep connected to "us."

LA–LAX. NYC–JFK. London–Heathrow. Chicago–O'Hare. These were ports of connection more than destination. I often felt I was going to miss a flight. And as in a dream where water grows heavier or air thicker, my body slowed and sometimes struggled to keep up. Someone was generally there at my arrival but the language, though English, was foreign: "If you're pre-checked you don't have to take off your shoes," I'm told going through the security check on a domestic flight to LA. How does having pre-checked my ticket make me less of a security risk, I never asked. Once arrived I put my bag quickly into the trunk of a friend's car at LAX as he tersely said he would be ticketed if I wasn't quick enough, adding, "If I were Black, I'd have a ticket right now." He was looking at the whistling policemen, who are Black. We spend most of the drive into the city speaking of how anyone Black has become a potential target. This is 2014 after Ferguson, but before the grand jury's decision not to indict the police officer who murdered Eric Garner; the assumptions of white supremacy still supremely assumed. My friend had a string of stories, Black people shot dead without so much as a provocation. He said a teenage boy lined up some Monster drink cans and waved down the police, saying, "Here I am here I am . . . you're probably going to shoot me now." And they did.

I was traveling away from the known—gripped by a vague dread and vertigo, a sense of life's end station where there would be no us—yet I carried wine with me in a communion between countries, and the body of the beloved to whom I was bringing it. I was not Mahmoud Darwish, the rapturous Palestinian poet of exile and love, but the wine was hard to carry and almost confiscated. At Heathrow I had forgotten to mention it was in my carry-on, sealed in its special plastic by the airport duty-free shop. It was also a metaphor of a certain kind of feeling, a love I wasn't sure would land me anywhere familiar. I knew, though, I wanted to arrive with the gift. "Freedom lies thereby in giving one's self one's own law . . ." (Stewart again), but my freedom came up against other laws too, and other essences, not least of which was the desire to arrive with wine. Doesn't desire create its own essence, a volition not always reflected in law, (i.e., anarchy, desire that exceeds law)? I was transporting so much desire in the wine I carried, and the law was going to trip me up.

"You'll be put on the next plane out," I was told when the plane was delayed leaving the Athens Eleftherios Venizelos airport. Interspersed with, "Everything will be all right," the general graciousness of the uniformed cabin attendees made for a recurring tenuousness, and paralysis—would I really make the connection? The wine slowed me down; the wine would delay me in the interminable terminal in the midst of the officious and indifferent.

There were fifty minutes to departure when we landed in London. I was given the red EXPRESS CONNECTION card and ran and ran and tried to still the panic as I sprinted through winding empty spaces of glossy ads and the lingering aromas of colognes and perfumes. The airline personnel were coolly professional. "Will I make the flight?" I say to one woman at a check-in point for transit. "We'll see," she says, looking at the screen, and then, "I think so." I notice the blank resignation on the faces of those in a hurry, sometimes a focused panic. The more impatient sometimes speak to themselves; a woman from Brussels in front of me and someone from Slovenia next to me had just come from Chicago where I was heading; I would make it if I was quick; I would make it if I didn't think too much about not making it. Breathing loudly and visibly out of sorts, I get on the airport bus to the gate when an Indian woman smiles my way. A man with a Scots accent is dismissive when I tell him of my EXPRESS CONNECTION. "That has nothing to do with security," he says. It is a word in so many of the refrains I hear. I will hear it frequently: "We want to secure your passage . . ." ". . . to make your comfort and security our priority . . ." "Please secure your seat belts and make sure your seats are in their upright positions."

It was two Africans, the one who said to his friend, "Let her go ahead," and a Southern couple who nodded and smiled as they saw the beginning-to-break expression on my face that made it possible for me to make the connection. I'd forgotten to say there was a bottle of wine in the carry-on that went through the X-ray band—it was quickly slipped off into the "To be Checked for Security" row and sat there as the minutes ticked past when I waved over a woman with her plastic-gloved hands, saying in barely controlled anxiety that I needed to have the bag checked as quickly as possible. The man with the Scots accent who had dismissed my earlier plea was now listening to the woman with her plastic-gloved hands. He nodded and pulled my bag from the group, taking it to another section where more women with plastic-gloved hands briskly opened it and pulled out the sealed bag with the packaged wine. "Keep it," I say, convinced this is the only chance I have to make the flight. "Really, keep it. I need to get this plane." And as I speak, I can't control the tears.

How melodramatic, I think, looking back at my scrawled notes in a calendar book I kept on the trip; it was probably melodramatic then too. I went to pull out the bottle with the intention of leaving it there when one of the young women doing her job said crisply, "You're not supposed to touch anything." I nodded mechanically and the director with the Scots accent said he would call the gate and let them know I was on my way. I asked one of the two women who checked the bag to tell me where the gate was. She repeated that I needed to take an airport shuttle. Looking at me intently, she said, "Listen carefully now," as the tears were quietly running down my face. "If you don't listen, you'll get lost and miss the plane." She spoke as if she was talking to an underage child. "Yes," I said, numb, yes, I thought as I ran and ran again through the crowded corridors of perfumes and airbrushed images of fashion models, numb and wanting with so much of myself to make the flight, as if this were the high seas off of Africa, the bordered coastlines of Sri Lanka, Syria, or the Aegean. Instead in this near-emptied airport space (after I make it through the duty-free shopping and up the escalators to Gate 32 . . . was it 32?), I asked (as if in a dream) a young woman next to me, "Are you on the flight to Chicago?" She nodded yes. "I lost track of time," she said, hardly flustered. I looked at her with my now sweat-glazed face and kept going, and then again after the escalator I ran some more. At the end of a long hallway of gate numbers and wide spaces there is a clutch of men who as I approached say my name as they take my boarding pass and let me board.

Excess

At night a light falls from two stories above the room we are staying in. The city is drenched in sounds. The room is an Airbnb rental in New York. The girls who are renting it to us are young yoga instructors and accommodating. We keep the window slightly open because they burn incense and it bothers us but we don't want to bother them. Outside the window there's a clatter of passing trucks. We talk of our excesses, of wanting to enter and leave the rooms we stay in with the least amount of luggage. The wine I carried across the Atlantic had made it, though I could so easily have dropped the bag and broken the bottle. I'm on a budget, so I carry my bag up and down the subway steps. A New Yorker friend wants to know why I don't "just pay for a cab." It's not a daily expense, after all. But even the smallest expenses are an expense—flavored water, for example, or unflavored water, anywhere from two-dollars-something to five dollars, depending on the flavor, or combination of flavors.

The expenses of travel astonish me; it's a lucrative business. From adaptor plugs to the tiny side dish of salad cheerily served to me at Heathrow for eight pounds. "You need it, you have it," the waiters and waitresses and shop assistants smile and nod as they promise fulfillment and happily take orders, while I watch those who seem to travel the lightest (and most expensively?) float through the Departure and Arrival halls, elegant in their bearable lightness of being. I wanted to know where the restrooms were at Heathrow. "Are you traveling business or first class?" one of the airport personnel had asked me. I blurted, "Second class," and quickly corrected myself, "I mean economy." But in fact I was traveling second class, my excesses were a burden and my desires exceeded me.

I read more of Stewart who writes of freedom as "bound to the fact of our status as living beings"; it is "the open decision to act in one way rather than another" that ensures the continuity of our living, she says. How nearly unbearable that decision can be. A headline in the *Guardian* announces Britain's decision to let refugee boats to their uncertain fates. Lady Anelay of the British Foreign Office believes there is an "unintended 'pull factor' in such rescue operations." That over time the withdrawal of search and rescue support would mean "word would get around the war-torn communities of Syria and Libya and other unstable nations of the region that we are indeed leaving innocent children, women and men to drown." According to Lady Anelay, this will provoke refugees to "think twice about making the journey." I wonder what she means by thinking twice; refugees risk their lives to flee their tragedies. It is 2014 and "Mare Nostrum," the Italian operation for search and rescue, had also been declared "unsustainable"; that language seems more honest; unsustainable isn't suggesting refugees might "think twice" about desperate journeys.

Streetlights flooded the rain-slicked air outside our room. That first night I felt impoverished. My bag was with me; my love was with me; the young yoga instructors had left us a bowl of fruit. An ambulance's red light briefly painted the long wall. The color was gone as fast as it had appeared. The wine didn't break or spill.

The undocumented travel the choppy seas for their thin freedoms, and I found myself overwhelmed in a room with conveniences, the wine drunk, and my love asleep.

Outside

"That will be $25 for checking in your bag," says the United Airlines attendant.

"Anything to make money," I say rather flatly. Her smile doesn't slip but it wavers. The shampoo and conditioner I'm carrying is in a 150 mL bottle so I will have to check it. Liquids over 50 mL are still a threat. There are holes in the foot of my stockings. I forgot to pack a belt or lost it. H&M had the cheapest and skinniest belt I've ever seen. It's plastic but looks like leather, and it's $1.99. I need, too, to get a better soap. These aren't necessities but the small choices in a large outside freedom. Probably nothing someone fleeing a country being devastated would think about.

I am comfortable. And I am not undocumented. I also need a razor and ask my love if I can use his. There seems to be no such thing as buying a single razor (the store I walk into has the cheapest in packs of six and ten). He gives me an extra that he has with him. He's had a nightmare. I say it's from reading all the news, the news that some like him choose not to ignore. "Everyone was killed," he says, including the girlfriend with him, and he could do nothing to stop it.

We leave the room to get some air and I buy stockings and the $1.99 H&M belt. People are quick to help. "Service" is a refrain, like "security"—"to be of service" or "to provide a service"—but the desire to serve will sometimes exceed the rules of compliance. The security women at Heathrow, for example, took the time to usher me through, repeating more than once where I had to go for my gate. The *FT Weekend Magazine* I read on the plane featured artificial intelligence and its role in changing the rules of our living; I took the issue with me. Our desires, in the way Stewart explains it, will no longer be "bound to the fact of our status as living beings" but to what one article called "a trans-humanist future"; the checkpoints and long corridors of our surveillanced worlds will begin to shape our desires. Kurt Vonnegut in *Player Piano* knew machines would change the world—and this was long before people began talking of the post-human.

Someone like Ann Miura-Ko, a young venture capitalist, says her biggest extravagance is "spending time with those I love." I kept the article for the word "extravagance" and made another note to myself. It is not a need but an extravagance for Ms. Miura-Ko to spend time with her family, something in excess of what she can afford in her busy work life. What will become the driving values of a world where love is an extravagance? It is an extravagance for me to cross the Atlantic to visit my love, to carry wine. But the excess gives me purpose, or volition, as Stewart might put it. Ms. Miura-Ko's mother, for example, according to what Ann Miura-Ko tells us, helped her succeed through her excessive demonstration of Ann's potential. When Ann failed her IQ tests and didn't get the scores to enter into an elementary school for the gifted and talented, she "would march in and tell them they'd got it wrong." Not anything a machine would do unless it was programmed for extravagant devotions; then again, who would the programmers be? Not mothers necessarily, or lovers carrying wine.

We buy pizza for very little money, read in bed, and talk of biometric technology. Or I talk of this since I'm reading an article in the *New Yorker* by Raffi Khatchadourian, who explains our inner worlds will become quantifiable. Detecting human emotion with cameras and other kinds of surveillance technologies will mean "*attention* will soon be as quantifiably valuable as money and time." There is something called "deep learning" that will give neural maps of information. I pause and write it down, and this sentence too: "Your face may also be your next wallet." Not good news for those whose wallets can only afford cheap H&M belts and pizza. Will the neural maps of the undocumented show the seabed of their tragedies? My love tells me the next big leap in innovation will be holograms. A presence will move around (be beamed into?) rooms "as if I was there," he smiles, and says we'll find each other in the virtual and intangible to make ourselves virtually tangible.

That night my dreams are terrible. I am taken by two of my closest friends in Athens to find my parked car. A self-satisfied man is telling me I need to fill in a document. I've forgotten what needs to be put into the spaces on the document, the ink is purple and I have to identify two pictures. I write "Daskale," which is the nickname of an anarchist friend; it means "teacher" in Greek. There's another picture too, though I don't recall if it was erotic, of a man I might be in love with. My love is speaking to me when I wake up. He tells me I was murmuring and crying. The worst part of the dream is when my two friends who helped me find my car tell me to follow their smaller car. I am relieved they will show me the way but almost immediately I hear a terrible sound. I've run them over. They're lying on the street, stunned, with the strewn parts of their car around them. They look at me as if still concerned for how I am. D's fingers are bent inside a piece of broken fender, two of her fingers cut in the middle like opened tubes. C's foot is mangled inside another metal part. I am calling out, "Oh God . . . Oh my God . . ."

"What does any of that tell you?" my love asks, listening.

"I'm losing my way . . ." I say, weeping, "and the violence . . . I can't control it." There is nothing outside that can't enter when you think about it.

Connections

You never know how what you are carrying will arrive. The fragility of travel is in its uncertainties. I watched anxiously for my luggage as bags toppled out of the funnel onto the revolving belt strap at O'Hare. A second bottle of wine labeled "King of Hearts" was wrapped carefully in clothing and bubble wrap; it could have bled its red through my clothing and suitcase while bags were tossed and piled on top of one another. Another extravagance, but when I saw the "King of Hearts" on a supermarket shelf in Athens, I couldn't resist bringing it with me.

Adam Phillips says, "Freud, as we know, was made anxious by traveling; and in the *Introductory Lectures* he associates journeys with death." I pulled my bag off the luggage belt with relish, relieved to find "The King of Hearts" had made it intact, though in the fragility is the foreboding. "Dying," continues Phillips, quoting Freud, "is replaced in dreams by departure, by a train journey," so "Travellers, whether they acknowledge it or not, are traveling toward death." Which makes connections all the more precious. I almost wrote "sacred"—maybe I mean that too. Preciousness, like the precarious, invites the sacred, a wine of both communion and death. When someone dies in Greece, we wish them *Kalo taxidi*," a "good trip"—as if our words might embody absence and ensure their safe arrivals.

So much depends upon the wish if not the arrival, like William Carlos Williams' red wheelbarrow in its rain-glazed glow, so much depends upon the changed perspective where the line breaks the "wheel" from the "barrow" so we can look into ever more generous space—"upon" or onward. It was a struggle to see beyond the rain-glazed glow of a difficult season. And the news was not good.

The wine label said "Canaan"; Galilee was where it was from, a biblical land of strife, precious and precarious, the wine offered to us by a neighbor in Chicago. A Palestinian youth named Kheir Hamdan had recently been killed in the village of Kufr Kana in Galilee, and the Adalah Legal Center for Arab Minority Rights called it murder. He had approached an Israeli police van, knocked on the windows with a knife. Police opened fire, then "dragged Hamdan's body . . . while he was bleeding and threw him into the van . . . instead of calling on rescue teams to save him." Hamdan did not travel far but the news of the killing did. As I drank the wine from Galilee there was a taste of death in the red. There is always a taste of death in the red. Stewart might call this a negative freedom; the taste of mortality, not a new way to experience the red of the wheelbarrow, for example. Negative freedoms speak of "inherent tensions between 'external' forces and 'internal' desires." Stewart says it best:

> . . . negative freedoms grant from the outset that power is something that must be wrested away from what is outside of our bodies and the limits of our bodily exten-sion. Positive freedoms, however, involve acts of affirmation—they are experienced not as away from but as toward. The prevailing theme of negative freedom is our mortality; that of positive freedom, our decision to live.

A movement toward is a movement of volition—though someone like Lady Anelay of the British Foreign Office believes this freedom is futile, and the open sea a det-riment if no rescue ships appear. Yet so much depends upon the open sea. So much depends upon the extravagance of ". . . our decision to live." Its excessiveness. Listen. It all started ferociously. I was dreaming of lettuce. I wanted to carry wine.

THE UNHOUSED

In her 1943 essay "We Refugees," Hannah Arendt explains the predicament of the suicide that "in their own eyes" feel themselves as having failed life's standard. Having given into despair in themselves, they die "of a kind of selfishness"; the failure of how to define, or redefine, one's self-worth given the loss of assumed standards makes for the quandary: "If we are saved we feel humiliated, and if we are helped we feel degraded." This quandary speaks to standards of citizenship and social belonging that in turn speak to systems of society and behavior that are radically reconfigured in the lives of displaced peoples. The refugee being a prime example of such, one that Giorgio Agamben in his 2008 essay "Beyond Human Rights" argues as "perhaps the only thinkable figure for the people of our time and the only category in which one may see today . . . the forms and limits of a coming political community."

I was learning of how standards are reconfigured in a year of working with Afghan families living in a school building in the center of Athens. My assumptions of dignity and belonging are changed as I am gradually invited into these lives. It begins with an invitation to have tea on the spread blankets that cover the floor of a classroom, where we leave our shoes at the blanket's edge. Mattresses are pushed up against walls; some pillows are on the floor. I'm urged to use a pillow as I am a guest but I shake my head, saying it's not necessary, only to realize this creates confusion and a look of disappointment, so I accept the pillow and drink the sweetened tea. I have a bag of raisins with me. There's a feeling of comfort and hospitality as we drink the sweetened tea and share the raisins. We discuss the fact that some of the children are attending the Greek public school. I'm asked if I will find a dentist for a three-year-old whose top front teeth have all rotted. It will be her birthday at the end of the month. It is not the date on her paper but the one her mother gives us in April. When I'd asked her father, he said he wasn't sure what the date was. But her mother knew it. We plan a party. I still have a string of lights with me, a cluster I'd forgotten to bring to the Christmas party we had in December. I plug them in and they start flickering; this makes Hennieh take a quick intake of breath and laugh. She keeps plugging and unplugging the lights as they flicker in their nest of color.

Changed circumstances will change how we see what we see. These small living spaces are made unexpectedly new. Even the city is made new. Omonia Square, where buses and metro stops make for intersections and gatherings, where information on squats, cell phones, fake passports, border smugglings, and plain old advice on everything from medicine to asylum petitions are hawked. It is also a world where Unés, one of the refugee children I've grown close to, notices things I've never paid attention to. He pauses in our walk along a crowded street as someone who is selling potato peelers loses his grip, and the peeler skids across the pavement; Unés picks it up, checks the blade, and gives it back to the man who is surprised anyone would pick up the now-broken peeler, and thanks him. We pause at a pet shop because one of the puppies catches Unés' attention. There's also a snake and a parrot on display. When we leave, Unés points to a huge ice-cream stand with its exaggerated plastic cone. I must have seen the thing too many times to remember because it sits outside the metro stop, but this time I see it as he does, and smile.

We speak a mix of English, Greek, and Farsi words, a jumble of emoji symbols, Viber and WhatsApp emoticons and letters. There is *salaam*, "hello," and *bedrood*, "goodbye." Thanks to the weekly games and books and songs in English that Alicia, Judi, Eirini, Stephanie, and other volunteers and donors have made generously available, some of the children are now speaking in near-fluent English phrases. We have become as familiar to them as they have become to us—Rocha, Hennieh, Unés, Narghes, Rakia, Azize, Maedeh; we know each other's names, even ages. Judi is asked why she isn't married, and if she was ever married. I'm asked if I have any children. One afternoon I show a video on my cell phone of couples dancing tango at the studio where I go. I'm asked if I do this too; Azize and her sister would like to come with me, next time I go. We go to a Luna Park where there are bumper cars and a Ferris wheel, and high-flying space-cars in which Hennieh, fearless, pushes on the gears so the air-borne car will go higher. She is giddy and I am anxious. Maedeh, who is fourteen, comes with me to a play my daughter is in. It is Ramadan and she asks her mother if she can skip the fast since she will be walking in the heat to the theater. Her mother is okay with this, and she dresses in white tights and her scarf and tells me you can tell the difference between Syrian and Afghan women by the way they wear their scarves. The Afghan women wear them more loosely around their heads, less tightly folded around their faces. There's a moment in the play when the top comes off one of the actors, it's a split-second; the actor is a statue that comes to life, her white, spray-painted breasts are bared. On our way back to the squat Maedeh will mention it, that the actor "lost her blouse," and I will nod and ask if she will tell her mother and she says she might, which makes me think I may not be invited to take her daughter anywhere after this, but then ask if it surprised or bothered her. She shakes her head and says, very simply, "This is Europe."

In his essay, Agamben references Arendt's point that one of the things the Third Reich ensured before Jews and Gypsies were sent to the extermination camps was that they had to be "fully denationalized . . . stripped of even that second-class citizenship to which they had been relegated after the Nuremberg Laws." Agamben is making the point that the concept of the nation-state founded as it has been on assumptions of citizenship and national belonging was a way to draw the line between which lives were "doomed to death" and which remained with human, legal rights. He argues the point first put forward by Arendt in relation to the Jews. He notes that "what is new in our time is [that] the growing sections of humankind are no longer representable inside the nation-state—and this novelty threatens the foundations of the latter." In other words, human rights as they have been historically tied to citizenship are now, as he explains, "Beyond Human Rights," an insufficient insurance, or reflection, of our humanity.

I get a message from Hennieh's brother, who is twelve, that her birthday party will be at 2:00, and would Judi and I like to come. Like the invitation to tea, I feel it's important to go, and want to celebrate my fearless four-year-old's day. I pick up a lemon pie that looks fancy and some paper plates, cups, plastic forks, party hats, and arrive after Judi. We're invited to sit on the floor in the classroom that is now the family's living space, the wide blankets are cleared, and what was once a school desk is brought in so Hennieh can sit there and blow out her candle. We'll wait for the guests, mothers, and their young children who arrive from other squats and camps, some from as far as Malakassa, where mostly Afghan families are housed; everyone arrives with a small gift, wrapped in colored paper. There are clips for Hennieh's hair, colored plastic bangles, a coloring book. There are balloons taped to the walls and the Christmas lights I'd brought are hanging from the blackboard where they have been taped. Hennieh has had her hair in tiny braids so that curls now fall around her face. Rocha puts new clips into it.

What is most impressive is the three-layered cake that's been prepared for the guests. My bought lemon pie, while delicious, is nothing compared to this chocolate cake, which Hennieh's mother, Azize, has made.

There is excitement as people gather. The women shed their veils and change into clothing that would make them indistinguishable from anyone else in the city. Sleeveless dresses, skirts, loose shirts with low necklines. Azize puts on makeup and earrings. When she wears lipstick, I think she looks like an Italian film star, but I'm not sure which one, maybe Monica Bellucci. There is music, and then dancing; the women pull me up from the floor where I'm sitting to join them; Rakia shows me how to move my arms in a slow wave; I start to laugh, feeling awkward, but then happy. The children are also dancing in a circle.

Judi asks me, "Who do you think is happier in a moment like this, a group of women in the UK or US or these women?" I say, without much thought, that I think right now this gathering is a happy one, and that everyone in the room is enjoying themselves. When Judi asks Maedeh why there are no boys, or men, she says they are never present at the women's parties but that they are not missed either. Judi asks if she wouldn't want a boy to dance with if she liked him, and Maedeh gives an emphatic "No!" and tells us that when the time comes, her mother and father will find a boy for her and will ask her if she likes him; if not they'll find another one. She says two boys waited for her sister, who is nineteen; "One waited for nothing" because Mina didn't want to go to him, and now there's another in Sweden. Maedeh is matter-of-fact, "If a boy wants to wait and I like him, then we can get married when we're ready."

We share stories, and our lives. When Maedeh speaks, Judi and I expect that she would wish to have some of the choices we in our Western worlds assume are the better ones, and find that's not the case; things are also less patriarchal, if more gender-specific, than we assume. For example, Narghes, who is also fourteen, tells me it is her mother who will pick the wife, or suggest someone, for her older brother, because her father is dead. She tells me her father had taught her to read and wanted her to learn languages. At some point in our conversations, I share an anecdote from Greek Orthodox weddings, that the liturgy uses the quote from the Bible about the wife fearing her husband, at which point the wife stamps her husband's foot in symbolic resistance. Azize and Maedeh look surprised and ask why a wife would be told to be afraid of her husband; I say, to remind them of who has the authority; they tell me both have their authority, but each has a different kind.

There are other ironies and surprises; that we communicate across language and culture in ways that reinvent our language and culture. My Viber messaging with Narghes was a mash-up of discourses and went on from our first month of friendship; from when she messaged me that she'd like a pair of black tights if I could find them for her to when the family moved to the Malakassa camp and finally got their papers under the family reunification law to go to Switzerland. We shared hundreds of texts, emojis, voice messages, in digital exchanges:

Bai Bai (Bye Bye)—Narghes writes; *Okey* (Okay); *You vato slip???* (You want to sleep???); *Hi you kam tomoro* (you come tomorrow); *Andrstan* (Understand); *vat taim you kam* (what time you come); *Hi you kam tomoro my mazr koking for you* (you come tomorrow my mother cooking for you); *Ined nmbr hosin and maide* (I need number Hossein and Maedeh).

The nation-state, says Agamben, is in demise; borders are being contested, people are being smuggled through at costs that sometimes include their lives; certainly the EU is in crisis, and the refugee influx has magnified what Agamben explains as the "unstoppable decline of the nation-state and general corrosion of traditional political-juridical categories." But as Arendt said of the Jews in 1943, "Refugees driven from country to country represent the vanguard of their peoples—if they keep their identity." These families, unhoused as they are from country and citizenship, are examples of this challenge; rather than feeling themselves as having failed life's standard, they show us how the standard is life itself, as in sheer life, as in what it means to continue with the traditions and values that shelter us.

Narghes' mother wants to give me a gift; it is a black patent leather bag someone has given her, and she thinks I might like it. She also ties up the bag of raisins I've brought because there are still some in the bag, but I say I want her to keep the raisins, and she says *tashakor* (thank you). My proximity to these lives has made the obvious newly tenable, and newly proximate.

TRANSITIONAL OBJECT,
A GRAMMAR FOR LETTING GO

*Initially, one's motives for translating happenstance
into acts of language may be quite private.*
—Nancy Mairs

It was a new job. My old job was defunct, like so many jobs in Athens. I was teaching "pointer words" and "connectors" to students who were uninterested, trying to explain the importance of structuring a sentence—but I was really trying to not fall apart. "Pointer words," "connectors," and "transitions" seemed an apt way to hold a sentence together and using language a good way not to fall apart. "Spot is a good dog. He has fleas," says the sample sentence, and the instruction: "Connect your sentences . . ." "What does Spot being good have to do with fleas?" asks the author. What does falling apart have to do with my standing in a classroom doing a job? The whole country was falling apart; the bodies of refugees were being washed up daily on the island shores of Lesvos, Samos, Leros, and Kos, and I was trying to concentrate on pointer words and connectors.

There's this about language and what we teach, or how we teach it, that it becomes a necessity to make sentences that make sense. It was a way to stay the confusion of what was not making sense. "You have coherence," the instructions continue, "when there isn't a loss of meaning, i.e., one sentence will 'connect' to another, and these will relate to one another when there is coherence." Transitions can help keep the relationship logical, and ". . . help you cross from one point to another in your text." I was trying to cross from where I had been deeply involved with someone to being no longer involved, to standing in front of a classroom of students uninterested in the lesson. Pointer words then, "this," "these," "that," "those," "there," are used to "point or refer backward to some concept in the previous sentence." To refer backward to when I'd wake to my lover's morning calls would make it hard to move on, a phrase as simple as *hey hon, I'm thinking of you* used to get me through the day. Though this was no sea, I had to accept that he was not going to be calling; if not equally terrifying, it was still terrifying.

In class I mention the refugees from Syria and Afghanistan barely managing their journeys as they reach the Greek islands, I use the pointer words: Then. They. This. There. I also repeat that the connections we make are what shape meaning. "Then I went to the supermarket. They were unkind. This is because I was without enough money to buy what I wanted. There was difficulty when I tried to explain why." The students are looking at me. I was, for once, more concentrated on them than the things my lover had said to me; one sentence in particular, *We need to remind ourselves to link arms through this*, had kept me looking back to how we might have gone from that point to the next: had we linked arms *then*, *there* might have been some possibility of getting through *this*.

I join a group of volunteers visiting a refugee shelter in Athens. We do activities with the children like making jewelry out of pipe cleaners, and give them magic markers and watercolors to draw and paint with. I don't know if that makes things worse or better. The children who smile and sing when we sing with them and who draw pictures and write their names in bold reds and yellows and greens are always happy to see us. But then we are gone, and they are left with the memory of our time together as if they were still in lives where drawing on paper with colored pencils and markers are part of a regular day. This was our intention: for them to feel some continuity with what had been left behind, or been taken from them, that we could still make these activities a part of their lives.

There's this about language too, that it is there to help us create continuities. The example in the grammar book goes on, "Spot is a good dog, *but* he has fleas," or "Spot is a good dog, *even though* he has fleas." The logic of syntax can be comforting in the way it will keep even the illogical connected. What does being good have to do with having fleas? Fleas, now a threat to goodness, will not stop Spot from being a good dog. These children we brought paper and paints and colored markers to have come from disasters I can barely imagine. When one of the older boys, a very polite sixteen-year-old, tells me that he will go to Germany, I want to touch him. He makes the statement so matter-of-factly I realize he's never questioned that this will be where he will end up. Maybe this is the country his family kept naming as they made the decision to seek another life, as their dinghy overturned in the middle of the Aegean and Greek fishermen rescued them.

He will go to Germany even though he is now in a squat with no papers, and the borders into northern Europe are closed. His English is better than some of the students I am teaching in a private college, and he is here living in the corner of a room with his cousins and an uncle where a curtain gives them some privacy. His name is Amir and he helps pick up the scattered markers and paper scraps after we're done with the activities. One girl wants to walk with me to my car. She won't let go of my hand, and I remember I have some tangerines and give her a couple. Someone from the group tells me I shouldn't have because others will want one, but she is happy and keeps smiling, and I feel somewhat desperate when I see her watch me drive away.

I have become fixated on the images of refugees getting out of dinghies or being carried onto the various island shores, the fluorescent orange lifejackets piled up on the shorelines with other assorted flotsam. I also read, "Holding someone's hand was always my idea of joy," from Clarice Lispector's *The Passion According to G.H.* and am haunted by that line when I stumble on the story of a young Syrian mother who is describing the loss of her eight-year-old daughter at sea. The line reminds me that holding my lover's hand really was one of the joys of being in love. The family had paid smugglers to take them from Turkey to Lesvos. Tarek, her husband, was with Linette, the younger daughter, and Lina, the mother, was holding onto Laya's hand when the boat capsized and she lost her grasp. "People were falling on top of me," she says, barely managing the words. I keep replaying the clip, listening to Lina's voice interrupted with sobs. She describes how they had not wanted to go into the boat but had been pushed at gunpoint by the smugglers. Tarek, who had said the boat was unsafe, was forced into it with others. His expression crumbles as he listens to Lina speaking and his palm wipes itself over his eyes. Linette, who might be six or seven, keeps looking back and forth between her parents, leaning against them and occasionally pressing her face into her father's arm.

I don't know how Lina manages to speak, but she is trying, I think, to speak of Laya so she is not forgotten in the numbers of the lost. "ONE death is a tragedy. One million is a statistic." This is the opening line of a *New York Times* editorial on empathy that argues against this to say empathy is a matter of choice. Syntax is consoling here too because syntax, according to the grammar book, uses transitions and pointer words "like an invisible hand reaching out of your sentence, grabbing what's needed in the previous sentences and pulling it along." I am back to imagining my lover's hand in mine but I am also determined to get through the lesson. Syntax can make coherences out of "an ambiguous or free-floating pointer"; to link an ambiguous "this" to a more clearly defined object, like "you." "This will affect you, too," I say to the class, referring to the lives of refugees. "This," I keep saying to myself, to keep present, to stay coherent.

An interview with Lia Purpura I read online feels like an uncanny, and thankful, coincidence of language. Though I haven't read the author or the book, I'm intrigued with what Purpura says about Jack Turner's *The Abstract Wild*. She quotes this: "A created environment is a neutered wild, a wild to which we no longer live in vital relationship"; it makes me think there is nothing of the "neutered wild" in the lives of the refugees, their wildernesses of uprooted, exploded lives is always vital. Purpura continues, quoting Turner, "To create a wilder self, the self must live the life of the wild, mold a particular form of human character, a form of life. Relics will not do, tourism will not do, books will not do." Purpura appreciates this, especially since she is a disciple of the word, believing "so wholly in language and books, frail as words are . . ."

Frail as words are, in this new teaching job, in my suddenly bereft state, I had to do certain things *even though* doing them could feel impossible. Maybe this was a reason I had become transfixed by the extraordinary ruptures in the lives of the refugee families I spoke to; they were teaching me something about fragility. They were the people a step away (or whole worlds away) from those of us in countries that were not at war, and still with jobs even if conditions had changed for almost everyone I knew in Athens. Maria made 200 euros a month, and it was black for weeks of eight-hour work days; Grigori was asked to sign papers saying he had taken his vacation leave but wouldn't be given any if he wanted to keep his job.

In another uncanny interface of language, Wayne Koestenbaum's review of Adrienne Rich's recently published *Collected Poems* has this line: "Her politics, not abstract, took place in blood vessels. Precarious ecologies stirred her sympathies"; the refugees' wild precarity is very much part of their journey in "blood vessels." Lifejackets and inflated boats are in daily Facebook updates. "At least 17 children drowned today, that's a whole classroom full," Alicia says in her FB status update. Alicia is regularly at the squat and provides supplies from readers to flip-flops, olive oil, and lemons.

I look up uncanny; it is from Freud's term *heimlich*, the word for homey or the familiar, and *unheimlich*, the word for the unfamiliar or uncanny, in his study about unexpected connections, an aesthetic of the fearful that takes over when what is unfamiliar becomes eerie. Koestenbaum continues: "Listen to her long vowels and keen consonants; listen to the leitmotif of pain." Listen to "the physiologies of words like 'crevice' and 'gobbets,' 'shearing' and 'vetch,' 'scours' and 'debridements,' 'pelt' and 'cumbrous,' 'juts' and 'bleak glare aching' . . . " Maybe Jack Turner's idea of a no-longer-vital relationship to his neutered wild is what Adrienne Rich was trying to salvage so wildly. She did remind us, "a wild patience has taken me this far." In the "bleak glare aching" of the difficult waking day I scour for a language to let go of what was once familiar. Pelt. Shearing. Juts. Connect what words take, what shearing will give back in its uncanny way, not simply in the body's cumbrous value. The smugglers (in 2015) are charging 600 to 800 euros per person, per body; "It doesn't matter if it's a child," Abeer says, who has made it from Damascus to Turkey, and then from Turkey to Lesvos and is now at the squat waiting for asylum papers to go to Berlin. Listen to the physiologies of the words, "It doesn't matter," a kind of transition as she articulates the matter of what matters, of words salvaged, "frail as words are . . ."

A colleague at school is going to Lesvos and asks for donations of "soft toys, like stuffed animals and teddy bears," which she will take with her to distribute to the refugee children. "Transitional objects" is a term D.W. Winnicott uses for those first possessions experienced in "the intermediate area," between an absolute dependence on the mother and the infant's gradual separation from her; an "in-between space" that he also calls "the holding environment." These objects are important for the infant's initiation into the world beyond the mother. A psychotherapist-pediatrician, Winnicott is interested in how a child learns to relate to the "not me" of the universe by using the teddy bear or blanket or doll or any object to enact an "object-relationship" of creative play and fantasy. This attachment becomes fraught when the environment is hostile. He names it "reality testing," that state "between a baby's inability and his growing ability to recognize and accept reality." At first I wonder what soft toys will do for children who have been in the midst of war and seen people drown, but then my colleague says she wants to take these toys because she remembers when her family left the island and moved to Alabama; she was five and a doll she kept speaking to was what helped her feel that she would one day return to the island.

One day at the squat, Aqdas, a fragile-looking Syrian girl, helps me pump balloons. She likes doing this and distributing them. The children all want one and are clamoring for them, but she speaks in a quick, strict Arabic and lines them up while she pumps one balloon after another and hands them out. I tell her that she can keep the pump, which pleases her. Each time I visit after that she asks if I brought balloons; I bring other things, coloring books and stickers, even a dartboard, but keep forgetting the balloons. We were told they were also winding up in the toilets, causing them to clog. But I do bring a packet some weeks later and ask Aqdas if she still has the pump. She motions that it's lost. I say I'll bring another one, which I keep forgetting to do. It becomes a kind of code between us. Every time I visit, Aqdas will say, "Pump?" opening her hands as if to ask "where?" Having forgotten it again, I shake my head and she laughs. When I leave there is always a question of the next day and time I'll be visiting, to which I gesture to help her understand "Thursday" will be the day after tomorrow. She shows me with her hands and expression that she understands we are skipping a day, and says, "Pump?" which makes us both laugh.

"Annotate key phrases," I am telling my students. "Highlight them: see how the highlights create a pattern; shape a meaning." How do we make sense when the connections fail, shapeless where there was something (someone) to hold onto? Lina lost hold of Laya's hand: does this mean she will keep trying to use words to shape what is no longer there? I am standing in front of my class and ask, "What are the key phrases and transitions?"—*Darling, are you there? Yes, hon, always here*—is what I hear, but read from the grammar book: "Ideally, transitions should operate so unobtrusively . . . that they recede into the background and readers do not even notice that they are there." Key phrases whose context has been ruptured in trauma will be repeated in new contexts, sometimes suggesting uncanny connections. As Anne Boyer points out, "There is trauma which is fantastic in the way it is brief and clear and also the way it lingers around and emerges unpredictably as if it will forever." I was speaking to students about how a sentence can bring parts together, that transitions and pointer words, "this," "that," "then," will create coherences. I was also remembering Abeer's feet, that she wanted flip-flops when we brought a bunch of them to distribute at the squat. She wanted a pair for her son, and for herself, and showed me her swollen ankles and thick-skinned heels. I also think of the young boy Abude reading on the sheet we spread over the concrete, and that the flies kept interrupting him. Abeer's classroom is its own kind of in-between space. I think of her as being what Winnicott calls the "good enough mother" who devotes herself to her students' need for a language that might help them into more hopeful lives.

I start to go more frequently to the squat, a school building, which is where Syrian and Afghan refugees—some 400, and lots of children—have taken shelter in what were once classrooms. There are as many as six families in a room. Some of the donations I sort through include a halter with sequins, high-heeled shoes, sexy underwear—not that they wouldn't be enjoyed, but I think these things as a good example of an ignorance of context, or indifference. On a scrap of paper taped on the wall outside the kitchen is a list of supplies needed; these include baby formula, olive oil, children's underwear, and flip-flops. We do simple activities with the children when we're not passing out donations. We bring scissors and glue, colored pipe cleaners, paper, and paints. We lay a bed sheet or two over the concrete of what was the school playground. Denmark and Switzerland have decided they will use the refugees' assets to keep them clothed and reinstated if granted asylum. On the Greek radio this morning there was a report that as many as seventy unescorted children are being put up in police stations in Athens. The journalist was saying there's no supervision besides the police and sometimes volunteers from groups like "ΤΟ ΧΑΜΟΓΕΛΟ ΤΟΥ ΠΑΙΔΙΟΥ" ("The Smile of the Child"). Some of the children had started throwing themselves on the ground and hitting themselves to get attention. At the squat they want to touch us constantly, hug, and sit in our laps.

I reread the *New York Times* piece on empathy. It explains that certain groups are less likely to feel empathy, one being "powerful people." They are like bordered countries with "less incentive to interact with others." The governments of Denmark and Switzerland are afraid the refugees will change the state of their states. Empathy would make them, and the rest of Europe, more porous, less familiar, more of *unheimlich* and eerie uncertainty. "Arguments against empathy rely on an outdated view of emotion as a capricious beast that needs to yield to sober reason . . . but this is not a deficiency in the emotion itself. In our view, empathy is only as limited as we choose it to be." I like this explanation that considers the "outdated" view "of emotion as a capricious beast." Perhaps my lover, like the Swiss and Danish governments, was afraid the beast of emotion might leave him with less self for himself, its uncanny shape-shifting effects too unpredictable.

In class I discuss this idea of digressing from the known on the level of the sentence. "Notice how we have used such connecting devices thus far . . ." and repeat, "this chapter, for example, opens with the transition 'And yet,' signaling a change in direction . . ." To make your sentences cohere you need to choose an appropriate connector depending on what kind of logic is at stake. The connections I am trying to make are multiple, as are their directions. I now enter two classrooms, the classroom that Abeer is trying to make of the basement room in the squat, and the classroom where I am teaching composition to paying freshmen who seem mostly uninterested; there is less of myself here than there is when I go to the squat, "and yet," I want to say, hoping to include more of what is "not me," more of what might be important to them, and say, "the transitions are important," and mean contexts have their own logic, which probably means, too, that my coherence is at stake.

When I go back to the squat, I learn that Aqdas is no longer there. I didn't bring the balloon pump, but I brought her a pair of leggings she had asked for and am told the family moved to the Ellinikon camp, which is much larger and where conditions are rougher. There are thousands at the camp. Alicia and I wonder if we should try to go find her. Someone at the squat says her family is in the process of getting their papers to go to Brussels. The children pulling at our arms, hugging us when we arrive or leave, reassures me that we are not unfamiliar, we are expected and welcomed, and there is always something that someone asks for.

Today one of the teenage girls says she would like hair dye and tells me she wants a blond color that is not too light because she shows me another girl's hair and says, "Like this." I start to make it a point to bring the more specific things I'm asked to bring. It is never enough. More women ask for hair dye, and when Maedeh's mother asks, and asks again, when I can bring the dye, I say, "Thursday." Today there were stories about Idomeni, the camp at the Macedonian border where some of the families have come from; one mother says a guard gave her food but wouldn't let her through; he is the border *guard,* after all, and yes, empathy is a choice.

A broken couch sits at the top of the steps where two men are sleeping, a girl is on the floor eating a flour wrap that looks like it's filled with yogurt; part of it falls and she picks it up with her fingers to eat. There's a plastic Christmas tree in the corner of the entranceway that no one has thrown out, probably from the days when the school was a working school. Abeer wants blank printing paper and whiteboard markers, and so I bring a packet of the paper and two markers from my college, signing off on supplies as if they were for my own classroom. It is not a place that looks like it can manage some 400 people, and yet there are that many people here and many babies. It doesn't look like it would be easy to concentrate on Abeer's lessons in the basement room either. The windows are small and near the ceiling and when it rains, as it did the previous night, there is water everywhere. But when I walk in with supplies and Abeer is talking to a woman in the flooded room, I look more upset than she does. She says she'll get a mop and asks if I managed to get colored tacks for her wall. She wants the thumb tacks "to make learning fun" and shows me how she will spell that phrase with the tacks. She also wants "biscuits for rewards," "ink for the printer," and "an English dictionary." Someone gave her a map and a whiteboard.

There are lots of flies today; the children keep scratching at what look like bites but are also chickenpox blisters. Abude wants to read and says words he mispronounces but keeps repeating. He doesn't pause at the periods or commas of a reader that describes locomotive engines; I wonder if he understands what he's reading in the speech bubbles that describe steam, coal, and electric locomotives. We are sitting on a sheet in a corner of the concrete playground and the flies keep interrupting his words because he pauses to move them away from his face and I do the same. He says, very proudly, that he is now eleven years old. "This," he says, showing me a speech bubble on the page, and I say, "This is a conductor. He drives the train. He is saying, 'Those gears control the speed.'" Abude repeats, "Those gears control the speed." I say, "He is saying..." and Abude repeats, "He is saying..." And I tell him we're going to have a birthday cake for him later.

My colleague returned from Lesvos after having taken the donations of soft toys. She was having a hard time piecing together what she had seen. A Kurdish mother showed her pictures on her cell phone of her two sons being shot. She had video-recorded the shooting. "This," she repeated in her bare English and told my colleague to "Sit. Eat." She was feeding her one surviving son, who my colleague guessed was around ten years old. She had made a bean dish on a gas burner she had on the ground, with the cell recording still on. "For you," she said to my colleague, who wasn't sure if she was referring to the video or the food. She could hear the gunshots. "The food was delicious," she said, and the Kurdish mother was "half mad . . . of course." "Of course" is another of the transitions suggested by the grammar book, in the category of CONCESSION words; others are "admittedly," "although," "granted," "naturally," and "of course." Although it's true this Kurdish mother was trying to communicate the trauma of her sons' murders, unlike Lina speaking of her drowned daughter, this mother was admittedly insane, or seemed so to my colleague.

I start to think grammar can become its own kind of holding environment, a space where ruptured continuities might find new ways to signify meaning. D.W. Winnicott explains that a transitional phenomenon enables an infant's separation from the mother, but that this can't happen "unless there is a good-enough mother," otherwise the child is afraid to part with its object which is then fetishized. Winnicott gives the example of the boy with the string, a seven-year-old "obsessed with everything to do with string . . ." joining together chairs and tables, but also his younger sister, who, Winnicott notes, was "the first separation of this boy to his mother." He explains the boy's anxiety as a result of his mother's depression and hospitalization when he was three years and eleven months old, following his sister's birth. This anxiety of separation is certainly part of what keeps the children so close to us when we go to the squat. They want to be held, and hugged, and always ask, as Aqdas did, when we will be back.

The boy with the string had exaggerated its use, says Winnicott, as "a *denial*" of what could make it "meaningless." *We need to link arms through this*, with its free- floating pointer, had left me unstrung; *this*, now detached from the promise of an arm linked into mine, had me thinking constantly of a time when an arm had been linked into mine. I could be like Abude and repeat the phrase and maybe, like Abude repeating "those gears control the speed," I'll listen to the sound of the words as they teach me of a new way to describe my reality.

I try to explain to Adube what it is he is reading. I gesture to show how different trains have different speeds and sounds. He suddenly uses a German word that I don't understand, but we laugh. Wayne Koestenbaum describes Adrienne Rich's "physiologies of words" as an attempt at salvaging meaning; to write that my hand in my lover's, or his arm linked into mine, promised to make bearable; whatever "*this*" might have been is part of the work of speaking and writing and the crisis of speaking and writing when meaning eludes it, like this eating, as my colleague ate, of what feeds us, this stringing together of what keeps coming apart. My colleague said she thanked the Kurdish mother who smiled and insisted she have more of the beans and rice. Abude tells me he is glad I brought this book on locomotives for him to read.

I am back in class, and use the grammar book's example sentence. A free-floating pointer can mean any number of things when unclear as to what the pointers are pointing out: "Alexis de Tocqueville was highly critical of democratic societies, which he saw as tending toward mob rule. At the same time, he accorded democratic societies grudging respect. *This* is seen in Tocqueville's statement that . . ." The grammar book notes it's unclear what *this* refers to, Tocqueville's criticism of democratic societies or his grudging respect; *this* ambiguity of language is a sly way of keeping open to possibilities, although the grammar book considers this a fault.

I am deliberately keeping open to the possibility of threading what might otherwise stay unstrung even if I can't always see the strands. "String can be looked upon as an extension of all other techniques of communication. String joins, just as it also helps in the wrapping up of objects and in the holding of unintegrated material," says Winnicott of the boy with his string. "I don't want to remember," Abeer tells me in the car as I drive her to the airport where she will finally go to be reunited in Berlin with her husband and older son. She bought a pair of espadrilles made of silver fabric for the trip and shows them to me. It's been over a year since she's seen her husband and older son.

Nothing was guaranteed at any point in the journey. Money given to smugglers, the wrong-sized lifejackets, some that didn't inflate, the boat to Lesvos that ran out of gas, towed to shore by Greek coast guards. Children had drowned; others had arrived separated from their families. "It will be a new life," she says, and I see her cheeks are wet but she keeps looking at the road and asks me about what she should expect in Berlin; will she be shown the way out of the airport, will someone tell her where to go? She has never been through an airport, having traveled so far by car, or on foot, or by boat. I say once she's through Passport Control her husband will be waiting for her. This is a strand of the story I thread for her, adding that I believe all will be well.

One of my students tells the class the story of Kunkush, the refugee cat who was separated from his family, a mother and five children fleeing war in Mosul, Iraq, when they arrived on Lesvos. Fishermen found the cat after the family had already moved on. An American volunteer, Ashley Anderson, saved him from strays and organized an initiative to locate the family. The drive cost 600 euros and was raised with a GoFundMe campaign. A local vet vaccinated the cat so he could be sent to Berlin where Anderson, with the help of Amy Shrodes and Michelle Nhin, started a "Reunite Dias" effort on social media, naming him Dias (Greek for Zeus) before they knew his actual name. I find this online:

> Nhin, who set up the Reunite Dias Facebook group wrote: "In a small way, his journey represents the plight of all who are seeking a better life. We need each other. If it wasn't for people taking notice of his vulnerable state and taking him in under their wings, he'd likely be fighting for food and struggling to thrive."

It was another uncanny moment, my student Eleni describing Kunkush's plight and reconnection with his family in Denmark, another example of the unexpected. I had asked the class to come up with topics for their writing assignments, and this was hers. I was now explaining transitions between paragraphs. We were back to pointer words. "Those efforts of the volunteers saved Kunkush's life," Eleni says. Students are taking turns demonstrating the application of a grammar exercise.

Someone talks of "creating flow" with pointer words and I become superstitious, thinking there must be a reason I keep hearing the phrase "like an invisible hand reaching out of your sentence . . ." When there is flow, when movement journeys us ("I don't like words like *always*," I'd said to my lover), we don't think of these things so consciously; "The hand is there," I say to the class, "when your transitions are building your ideas, but don't take that hand for granted." They laugh. They are going to pair up and read each other's drafts. I want them to group "a constellation of key terms and phrases, including synonyms and antonyms." According to the grammar book, this will clarify their strategy for relating the points of their argument to each other. My key terms include "empathy" and "wild"; possible synonyms are "connect" and "uncanny"; possible antonyms, "rupture" and "border."

THE PARTS DON'T ADD UP, AN ASSEMBLAGE

These were the anonymous lands that you called home,
because they needed to be called something, if only for a moment.
—Geoffrey Nutter, "The New Atlantis"

Embedded in the word refugee is refuge, a place of specificities, a place like home, which includes a sense of the familiar and tangible, until these locations are also (dis)placed.

The refugees in Greece, caught in the impasse of a closed border since March 2016, have had to relocate in hopes of finding their way into northern Europe; the Afghans in particular have been told they don't have the option of seeking asylum, their escape from their war-torn country not—according to the European Union

(EU)—analogous to those of the Syrians. The Former Yugoslavian Republic of Macedonia (FYROM) was one of the first countries to reject the Afghans after the March 2016 agreement between the EU and Turkey effectively closed the borders out of Greece.

According to the Danish Refugee Council, the number of killed and wounded civilians in Afghanistan in 2015 was the highest since 2009. Several countries that lie on the route from the outer borders of Europe to the rest of the continent have built fences or introduced border controls, which aim to reject a certain number of nationalities. "I visited Lesvos in Greece last week and have met some of these vulnerable people that now cannot continue their search for safety," says the council's International Director, Ann Mary Olsen.

The Afghan families who occupy the abandoned school building in central Athens are together with Syrian, Kurdish, Turkish, and other refugees. The experience of shared space is new to them, as these groups have not mingled historically. People who would not otherwise live together are now living together. There is this about survival and its necessities in an urban metropolis: one discovers new ways to be.

The writings of Hannah Arendt, who coined the phrase "the banality of evil" about the rise of Nazism, whose *On Totalitarianism* provided groundbreaking observations regarding the leveling apparatuses of totalitarian regimes, remind us that intimacies are rooted at the heart of every human situation. The heart is a porous border, a mutable location: ". . . the intimacy of the heart, unlike the private household, has no objective, tangible place." Unlike constructions of nationhood and government, the life of refugees reminds us that what is constructed can come undone, and in the undoing, the devastated are also sites of beginnings.

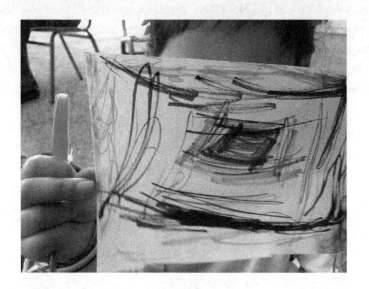

"When FYROM closed its border for the Afghans, [it was] yet another symptom of what we see happening in many places in Europe. People have the right to get their asylum case processed—and not be rejected based on their nationality. It is not borders that need protection—it is the refugees," says Danish Refugee Council director Olsen. The Somali-British poet Warsan Shire has made her poem "Conversations About Home (At a Deportation Centre)", famous with lines such as, "No one leaves home unless home is the mouth of a shark. I've been carrying the old anthem in my mouth for so long that there's no space for another song, another tongue or another language."

Another language spills over in the Athens squat, where phrases are repeated that are new to me, such as *tashakor*, "thank you" in Farsi. *Tashakor, tashakor*, says Azize, who is from Bamiyan. We communicate in gestures, language pieced together with nods and smiles. It makes for a space that bridges what we don't know how to say. I have brought tea bags and some honey, but Azize is especially happy for the hair dye that will turn her hair blond. And while I am the one who has come from an apartment of my own and a full-time job—the kinds of things they have escaped their devastated country to find—I am the one who feels nurtured. I sit for the tea they offer me on the five-blanketed floor that has become a living space. But there is a surprise, because Narghes, who is fourteen, wants to use the tea set someone gave her as a gift. She tells me to wait as the boys are playing a dart game next to us. She wants this to be a special moment between us, the girls, including Hennieh, age four. So I sip my tea slowly, and when the boys leave, Narghes brings out the tea set.

We are now in this frame where what lies outside its borders, what could undo the tenderness of the moment contained here, is forgotten. Only the present fits in and it is a refuge; this present, which Homi Bhabha has theorized in *The Location of Culture* is where the subject finds itself "in the moment of transit . . ." What lies in the "*beyond*" of this present is "unknowable, unrepresentable . . ." While Narghes pours the tea into her dollhouse tea set, we enact a homemaking ritual, precarious for its liminality in a space that was once a school room, now where families sleep, cook, eat, and live out days, weeks, and months, using the electricity and water that has not been cut off by the municipality. There is an unspoken understanding that if the refugees did not have the option of occupying these abandoned buildings in central Athens they would be on the streets, and the municipality under Greece's Syriza government has accommodated their needs. Like Narghes with her tea set, a home is made of what's been found or given. The present is not part of any sequential temporality but a reflection of what Bhabha calls our "proximate self-presence," which reveals our "discontinuities . . . inequalities . . . minorities."

Like cities in wartime, resources have become scarce in austerity-ravaged Athens; its gutted economy makes for a renewed appreciation of the existence of refugee squats, of alternative and collective ways to share resources. The city's shuttered stores and buildings, left to deteriorate as a consequence of the financial crisis that began in 2009, have visibly altered the city; these are the spaces that are being reinvented by refugee communities. People who didn't expect to be here, some of whom still hope to leave, have nevertheless, out of necessity, transformed parts of Athens. Now, too, a group who were once students in this school building comes each Friday to cook a hot meal for the families. They ladle out soups and stews from large pots on burners they've set up in the playground, also thankful that their school building is no longer rotting, but is instead sheltering lives.

"I don't know what we're doing," one of the volunteers says of our small group who visit the squat. She continues somewhat critically to say here we are with our coloring books and packets of crayons and magic markers, and here they are with their experiences of near-fatal voyages, living on handouts and floor spaces partitioned by layered blankets. It is a question of scale and perspective, what Bhabha describes as the interstices of broken certainties. A place "in-between" what was once known and is now unknown, will "take you 'beyond' yourself to return, in a spirit of revision and reconstruction," to a present which keeps changing and which keeps you in motion.

Warsan Shire writes, "*They ask me* how did you get here? *Can't you see it on my body? The Libyan desert red with immigrant bodies, the Gulf of Aden bloated, the city of Rome with no jacket.*" A city with no jacket, Rome no less, with its history of empire, and empire's oppressions collapsed to the fact of someone without a jacket. The metaphor reconfigures a hierarchy, bringing down the edifice of history that makes of an emblematic city a body inadequately clothed and vulnerable. In the poet's personal imaginary, the detail is resonant, captured in the mind's or camera's eye the fleeting (and fleeing) movement that got her *here*.

"And all rulers are the heirs of those who conquered before them," the philosopher and urban essayist Walter Benjamin wrote. "Hence, empathy with the victor invariably benefits the rulers." His famous angel of history is something of a conundrum, as he would like to "awaken the dead and make whole what has been smashed . . ." but he is fixated on the wreckage, the "pile of debris before him [that] grows skyward." As a storm is blowing into his open wings, pushing him forward with his back turned to the future, Benjamin famously notes, "This storm is what we call progress." This storm—*can't you see it on my body?*—has no borders, but for the names we give it. Radical displacement can subvert the circumstances that have diminished its victims—the debris of devastated cities, the emptiness of abandoned spaces are also unexpected, porous sites. It's a question of how we name the parts that move us.

War—

hums, *I will make love*

to you in a bed of blood and faith,

will show you her lips,

hide her teeth, her money-scented

breath, the rust of her tongue, the children

underneath her fingernails.

> —Zeina Hashem Beck,
> "Naming Things (*for refugees, Sept 2015*)"

~~LEFT BEHIND~~ FOR A SQUARE OF SPACE

Any good magician or psychoanalyst knows, it's the deliberate chalking of
a particular square that allows for the discovery of personal order and
private mythology.
　　　　—Rebekah Rutkoff, *The Irresponsible Magician*

2016

You ~~leave what you know,~~ leave your shoes at the rim of the blanket or sheet. This is what Hennieh does, slipping off plastic clogs to step onto a sheet placed over the concrete. I haven't bothered to unlace my boots (it's November). I sit so they don't touch the fabric. Scattered crayons, drawing paper, colored pipe cleaners used to make rings and bracelets, children's books; a world covers this square of cloth.

~~In what used to be a schoolroom,~~ Azize and her family live on one side of a hanging sheet where I meet Maedeh. Some families lucky enough to get relocation papers for Sweden, Switzerland, Germany will move on—northern European countries equal an imagined future, a past ~~left~~ for a tomorrow.

It's Hennieh's fourth birthday. "Mama Hennieh," Maedeh and others call Azize who crouches in a corner of the blanketed floor to put on makeup. The lipstick's red lights up her pale skin. "Mama Heni," says Maedeh, or "Mama Maedeh," says Azize when she speaks to Saliha, Maedeh's mother, both women in their early thirties. First names are less important than the bonds that transcend ~~singularities~~. Months later Azize will say she's forgotten ~~Saliha's name~~ when I'll ask how she and Saliha address each other over Messenger and Viber, the family now in Sweden; they call each other "sister"—*xocharn*—at least this is how the word sounds to me.

A windowpane falls out of the schoolroom wall as randomly as a bomb ~~explodes in war~~, and the pane almost hits Azize, but we grab it, matter-of-factly. For Hennieh's birthday party Azize tapes a cluster of blinking Christmas lights to the blackboard for decoration but the tape isn't strong, and ~~the cluster~~ keeps falling. She left Bamiyan ~~where she is from, left a home, her mother, and two sisters,~~ to get to Iran.

Rakia's pregnancy is starting to show. She raises three fingers to say three months. When we gather in the sheeted-off space ~~where there are no men,~~ she takes off her headscarf to dance. Maedeh finds music on her tablet. Her headscarf comes off too. Some of the women have changed into dresses with low necklines, others with hems above their knees, but it's the lengths of hair ~~that I haven't seen,~~ and the colors the hair dyes have streaked in blonds and reds that are startling. Everyone looks a little punk. Hennieh's four-layered cake of chocolate, biscuits, orange, and strawberry slices sits on a tray. My store-bought meringue pie is pretty and Hennieh and Azize like it, but ~~it doesn't feed as many,~~ the three-tier cake baked in a portable oven is enough for everyone.

Maedeh finds the music and Rakia lifts me off the floor. She takes my hand, sways her shoulders, motions me to follow. ~~I'm self-conscious.~~ Rakia smiles as I move my shoulders. We're in a circle of women whose ~~usually covered~~ hair lays newly brushed over their shoulders and backs; it falls into their eyes and gets caught in the corners of their mouths as we dance and laugh.

"Where are you from?" a woman asks in English. "Here," I say, "my father is Greek, my mother American." She says, "You are Greek, ~~it doesn't matter where your mother is from.~~"

Outside ~~the sheeted partitions,~~ the uncovered floor, scattered shoes, a freezing hall-way. Closed classroom doors keep in what heat is made of space heaters and layered blankets. It's more heat than I expect. The windows are sweating. Wires from the multi-socket power strips lay tangled up across the floor. A woman is weeping, opens her mouth to show me a tooth. A woman is rocking on the balls of her feet which look painfully chapped. There are up to five and six families in a ~~class~~room and lots of blankets. The space heaters are small, the rooms have high ceilings, but the walls are thick.

My fourteen-year-old friend Narghes lives in #14, one of the rooms where up to twenty-eight people have slept: now it's two families. Narghes' family includes her mother Malihé, her twin brother Unés, Ibrahim, her fifteen-year-old brother, and her grandmother Fatima. Music, coughing, plates being stacked in basins, cell-phone chats, float between ~~the sheeted-off~~ spaces. Plates and pans and clothes are washed in the schoolyard sinks. Old faucets spew water ~~the municipality has not cut off.~~ Pigeons gather. Mar says, "Flying rats," and shudders. But the children are delighted when the birds ~~cluster and~~ take flight.

The first time Azize invites me into her floor space she's anxious I might not ~~take off my shoes,~~ respect what has become a living space. Parameters make specific what lies ~~within~~ them: "Bring for me glitter?" Maedeh asks. She is going to the local Greek school in Exarchia with Narghes, Ibrahim, Unés, and Amir Houssein (Azize's eleven-year-old son). The glitter, like hair dye, aspirin, dentist visits, shoes, hair tonic for lice, antibiotics, ~~are some requests that~~ begin to contour my day. Maedeh wants the glitter "by Friday" for the school Christmas party. I want to get the fancy four-cylinder container available at the all-purpose JUMBO store. Alicia wonders, "Can it wait for tomorrow?" ~~But tomorrow is Friday.~~ "Can we stop by the school to drop off something?" she asks her husband over the phone. He wants to know what's so important that it can't wait ~~for tomorrow~~. It's eight in the evening. She says, "A container of glitter for one of the girls," he ~~almost~~ hangs up.

The families have ~~left homes in~~ other lands: Rakia, twenty, and Mohammed, twenty-four, with their seven-month-old Asma, came from Iran ~~to Turkey to Lesvos~~ to Athens. Saliha, or "Mama Maedeh," has a soft spot for Asma. She rolls Asma over pillows and Asma laughs. She buys a single sweet every day from the corner kiosk to give her. Rakia talks to me in gestures, some French, a smattering of English. She will show me a tin ~~of baby cream~~ that's empty, I'll bring her something for diaper rash and she'll nod thank you. ~~Another day~~ Maedeh tells me her brother is in Sweden, that he's fourteen and walked twenty-one days to reach Germany once he made it to the Macedonian border, then Sweden ~~when the border was still open~~. The family is waiting for relocation papers; ~~a year and a half will pass of living in the classroom~~ when the papers come through, ~~a total of~~ almost three years from the time they last saw him ~~will~~ have passed.

Moha explains the EU family reunification policy allows for an underage child (under eighteen) to request their mother ~~but this no longer involves all family members~~. He will be relocated to Germany ~~after leaving Damascus, after being taken to an ISIS camp where he was almost shot~~. Moha helps out, translates, reads poetry, wakes the kids for the Sunday morning dentist appointments. His mother will die in Syria ~~before a chance to travel to him~~. He will file for relocation ~~after considering, like many, making a go for it at the border~~. Offered a full scholarship to finish his degree in English ~~(which he was studying in Damascus)~~ at the American College in Athens, he will have signed his papers for Germany already ~~and will regret he didn't know of the scholarship in time~~.

Narghes shows me the Swiss flag above a café in Geneva on her cell phone. Her brother took a selfie when he made it to Switzerland ~~as the borders closed~~. He is now seventeen. "Family connections," Narghes says as if she's been practicing the phrase, when I ask how they found him. It's a phrase she repeats, and "Katehaki," where asylum requests and relocation petitions are processed in Athens. "They say no," Narghes says, pointing to Fatima, her grandmother. The Swiss government has given their okay to Malihé, Ibrahim, Unés, Narghes, ~~but not Fatima~~ for relocation. Fatima crouches at the edge of the sheet where the children draw and paint and concentrates on filling in the wings of butterflies and flowers.

Narghes says her mother would like hair dye. Ibrahim tries to explain the color she wants, "a little bit olive, little bit aubergine." He shows me images ~~of vegetables~~ on his cell phone, and points to an eggplant.

The layers of five or six blankets donated by UNHCR make the floor soft. Someone is singing. I am sitting with Maedeh's family when Azize comes in with Hennieh. We cut the Xerox copies of photographs Eirini and I have taken. We hope the pictures become a memento of ~~the school and~~ our times together. Malihé offers us tea, or chai, and chocolate wafers.

2017

Your expectations ~~are~~ changed~~; you take for granted~~ being seated, ~~having a surface for~~ arranging a hairbrush, hair clips, loose change, becomes newly important. You realize this when Hennieh's eleven-year-old brother, Amir Hussien, says it's hard to sit for long periods cross-legged. When you go to a Luna Park on a Saturday morning, the first of the new year, everyone grabs a seat on the metro, their stiff plastic backs are welcome. You bring your daughter's American Doll to Hennieh; the doll's name is Felicia; the doll has a four-poster bed, and Hennieh sleeps on a floor mattress. I ask Hennieh to give ~~Felicia~~ an Afghan name, and she calls her Kimia, ~~the word for~~ chemistry. The next time I visit, I see Kimia's bed ~~has been turned into~~ a side table where Azize has placed jars.

Nirgina is new to the squat; she arrived with her six-year-old daughter Naz and is painting henna designs on ankles and calves and the backs of hands when I meet her. She offers to do the same for me. I marvel at the steadiness of her hand as she draws with the tip of a paper cone. She says the henna ~~is not good, and~~ will fade in a few days.

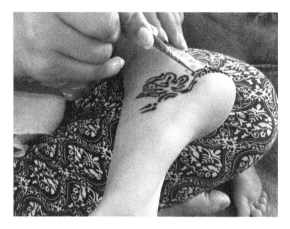

She left ~~Kabul~~ with Naz because her husband "was bad." Her mother is in Sweden with her father and older brother; ~~in Kabul she had been~~ a schoolteacher, ~~taught "Oxford English." Now~~ she wants to get to Sweden ~~because there's "no work in Greece . . ."~~ I say she could teach English, be paid for her henna designs. She will get herself to Sweden, she says, with the help of smugglers. "But they are expensive . . ." I say, "also dangerous." She nods, concentrating on the design she is making on my hand. I repeat she could make money doing this when she says quietly, "It's for free."

I offer Nirgina English language books; this is ~~more~~ to do with my ~~feeling of~~ helplessness, ~~trying~~ to imagine ~~a solution,~~ alternatives, when Nirgina says she finds free English lessons on YouTube. YouTube is where Hennieh finds nursery rhymes and videos of kittens, and Mina checks for recipes. Nirgina tells me ~~there is no future for her in Greece;~~ if she can't manage to get herself and Naz to Sweden, she'll send Naz with a Pakistani family.

A series of emojis turn up on my Viber from Narghes—a weepy face, a shocked face—the line, "Unés go!" another weepy face, then, "vat taim you kam???" ~~I don't understand.~~ I text, "I there in 1 hour!" and leave for the squat. My syntax pared down to ~~some belief that~~ fewer syllables ~~makes for easier understanding.~~ Narghes answers, "Okay god god vere god"; while I know "god" is "good" and "kam" is "come," I learn urgency becomes its own syntax ~~and grammar~~. Narghes' twin brother Unés was ~~left~~ on the metro platform as the subway doors closed and he was separated from Malihé and Narghes.

Unés is taken to the children's hospital ~~picked up by the police~~. Narghes' thirteen-year-old twin has a difference, an acute intelligence sometimes made fun of. He knows the side streets from Omonia Square ~~when I am lost~~; he knows to unknot the tangle of my jacket strings ~~when I'm ready to cut the fabric in frustration~~; he did something mysterious to fix my cell phone ~~that had frozen~~. But his fifteen-year-old brother Ibrahim is bullish with him. "Unés' brain is this," Ibrahim says, showing me a pebble when we're on a walk. Unés understands the insult and pushes him. Ibrahim hits him back when Malihé intervenes in rapid Farsi. In the first days of our visits Unés ~~swipes the markers, scissors, socks then~~ gleefully shows me the markers, scissors, and socks he's hidden; it's a game. When I ask for things back, he gives them ~~until they disappear again~~. Sometimes I see a hardened expression on Ibrahim's face. Other times ~~it breaks into~~ a fabulous smile. He wants me to print out the reams of photographs he sent over Messenger after Eirini and I turn up with stapled paper booklets to glue in pictures.

A sheet or a blanket marks a boundary—where the sheet or blanket ends are the imagined places beyond ~~mattresses on the floor, pushed against walls, crates for shelf space, planks to place suitcases, pots, plates, cups, pillows, clothing, beyond the coughing and snoring and drifting harmonica sounds, the hallway where Narghes chips her front tooth falling off a skateboard~~, where Hala has a pet, a table and chairs and food on the table.

We ~~leave to~~ find Narghes' apartment, whom my friend Narghes, with the same name, tells me is "a good girl"; ~~we are lost~~ in the backstreets that cut across to Exarchia, her family lives in an apartment rented for them by PRAXIS, a Greek NGO. They both go to the Greek public school with Maedeh and Amir Hussein; Narghes wants Narghes to come with us on the trip that Judi has planned to Rhodes. I discover parts of the city ~~I haven't seen before~~; stop at an ATM, make a point not to cover the numbers as I punch in the digits. Narghes watches, then says, "People say no look." I explain the code is to protect the person's account ~~but I'm uninterested in my explanation~~. I'm interested in what trust might mean in lives that find themselves in the corner of a classroom because cultures ~~from countries that have been destroyed~~ continue to dream and survive.

Narghes' friend Narghes ~~doesn't wear a hijab,~~ leaves her shoulder-length hair loose.

Narghes tells me this before we arrive. When Narghes' family first came to Athens, Malihé wasn't strict, but Narghes says her mother now wants her to cover her head when she goes out. "We don't know her," Narghes' mother says in soft-spoken Farsi, referring to me. We are asking if she will let her daughter come with us. My Narghes says her friend Narghes' family knows her, and she knows me, "for a year now"~~, as if this should be enough for the family to entrust their daughter to strangers going on an excursion~~. Narghes' mother excuses herself to speak with her husband in another room; ~~they don't know me, but~~ I'm invited into their kitchen. Narghes and I leave our shoes at the entranceway and are offered water and chai. I sit with the two chatting fourteen-year-olds. When Narghes' mother returns she tells Narghes they will allow their Narghes to go on the trip if the contact person at PRAXIS gives their permission.

I bring Maedeh sweatpants and ask if she's seen Narghes. They are in another spat ~~and aren't speaking~~. When I find Narghes in her room she's upset. Maedeh keeps boasting of her high marks in school; Ioanna and Argiris, their young Greek schoolteachers, give Maedeh stars and encouraging comments. Narghes says she doesn't like math. Judi says Maedeh is the more secure of the two because she has her father. Malihé, Narghes' mother, was married at twelve. Ibrahim tells me this with a short laugh. Narghes shows me a picture on her cell phone, a child with makeup. The makeup looks garish. ~~The picture upsets me but~~ I smile. Unés is asleep on a mattress after his metro escapade.

Malihé is not being treated well, according to Narghes. An Afghan woman alone means a woman who is half ~~seen~~. And Ibrahim refused~~, when it was his turn,~~ to clean the toilets at the squat. Ibrahim wants to hang out with attractive girls and the cool boys. I get over thirty pictures over Messenger from him, pictures of him looking Brando-like with the smiling girls. I'd brought photo albums for Narghes and Maedeh hoping they will remember this time; Maedeh says she will ~~always~~ remember.

Images from Narghes pop up on Viber—"pants for cold," a winter coat with a rim of lavender fur. She's fourteen, after all. I'll say the lavender-rimmed coat is "expensive," ~~I tell her my own coat is a couple of years old~~ she'll nod, "If no money never mind," she says. I take her and Maedeh shopping during the winter sales. I want to reconcile them. Narghes will ask, "Expensive?" as we pull clothes off racks and she and Maedeh go into the dressing rooms.

Space will reconfigure its occupants as much as being reconfigured by them—take any mapping, take the once-indigenous North American continent occupied and remapped by a cluster of Calvin-inspired fanatics. Take the fact that that group in-spired a nation that pushed First American groups off their lands and formed reser-vation camps. Today casinos are one of the ways these reservations fund themselves. The current Greek prime minister wants to open casinos on islands and tourist hot spots to generate tax-free incomes, as an economically imploded Greece has become something of a reservation within a larger Europe. Hot spots, a term given to refugee camps first supported by organizations such as the UNHCR, suggests some ways boundaries engender value. Like a reservation, a camp, a hot spot, the terms of habitation become dependent on what organizes them.

On the floor in room #14 Saliha, Azize, Rakia, Mina, Nirgina, Maedeh, and others have organized clusters of bud-like dough pouches to celebrate Eid and the end of the Ramadan fast. It takes three bus rides to another part of the city to borrow "a poot," Maedeh says. They got it from one of the shelters. I eventually understand

"poot" is the five-tiered pot that the dough pouches are steamed in. We spend time
filling and shaping the dough, separating them into batches on a square plank ~~from
a broken cabinet.~~

Nirgina finally sent Naz with smugglers. It cost 4,000 euros. They provided a false
passport and passage with a Pakistani family whose daughter she was supposed to
be. "It was the only way," Nirgina tells me, and sees me beginning to tear. "You cannot ~~cry,~~" she says very seriously. She, the mother, has cried since Naz left ~~but they
had been turned back several times when the two of them tried to cross together.~~
Two days later Naz arrived in Sweden. She was given "good clothes and food." But
she wants her mother. "We have not been apart for more than ten minutes," Nirgina says, and shows me Naz on her cell phone, now in Sweden, dancing in a dress
gifted by her grandmother.

We, the spectator, visitor, we who occupy our framings of meaning suggest a language that arranges sentences, that becomes its own sentence ~~of meaning~~. And for
those outside the frames, to smuggle in their meanings, to make a space for what is
excluded is to reconfigure ~~the parameters of~~ geography and time.

2018

A young Pakistani boy takes my hand. "I want a medicine," he says in unaccented

English with a large smile. A spray for lice is written on a slip of paper the pharmacist refuses to give ~~without a prescription~~. We get shampoo and hair tonic instead. On the way back to the squat he tells me, "In Pakistan they took my father," ~~who was~~ "tall like me." The boy is no more than twelve. When he says he "hates them," I touch his shoulder, "You are here, and your father is ~~somewhere~~ thinking of you and happy that you are here."

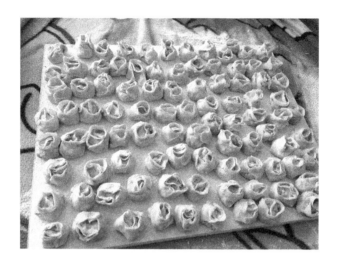

Allison Cobb writes, "The truth is that shelter always eventually fails—the tiles crack, a fire starts, the ants thread their nests through walls" (*After We All Died*). The truth is that the distance of countries is ~~collapsed~~ in our messages to each other, a shelter of words bridging ~~distance~~. The moment a home is called home it can be taken ~~apart~~ elsewhere. The floor is visible for the first time when Mina peels off the gray UNHCR blankets to wash them. Under the blankets that carpet the mosaic tile, we see broken and chipped pieces. She is preparing for Eid; now-sweet smelling sheets and blankets dry on a rope in the hallway. No, ~~she didn't go for English lessons in Khora, the place giving free lessons and food,~~ "No time," she says, when I think it is time they have, time that becomes more ~~theirs~~.

I meet Azize and Hennieh on a bench outside the Paidon hospital for three months of dentist appointments. They take two buses from the Eleonas camp. I ~~leave my school between classes and~~ find them on the same bench next to a kiosk; Hennieh's rotting teeth will be fixed by Olina, a young intern in the dentistry school who puts on cassettes of Greek children's songs so Hennieh ~~will be less afraid and~~ might concentrate on the songs. I buy her a mermaid doll from the kiosk, and a stuffed animal to hold.

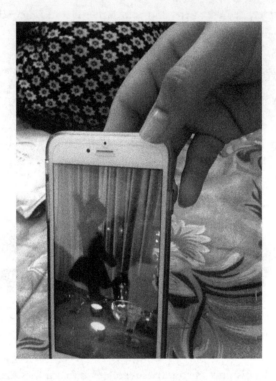

It is the dentist visits that stay with me. And Maedeh writing from Sweden to Azize in Athens to meet me at the Paidon hospital for Hennieh's appointments, Maedeh translating ~~what Azize does not understand of~~ my English. It is Azize's carefully tied bows and ribbons in Hennieh's hair that I ~~still~~ see.

Do they keep these pictures, as I do? The one from when we went to the Luna Park? Azize had a colored photocopy I had given her. Hennieh and I at the Ferris wheel, the mothers with their arms around each other, Azize's sister with her son, Taha. My daughter holding Hennieh's hand. Did these pictures make the world more habitable? Amir Hussein asked if I could send pictures over Messenger. Azize wanted to remember. I want what's been left ~~behind~~ of those days, Hennieh holding the kiosk-bought toys so she would ~~not~~ think of ~~anything as Olina worked on her teeth but~~ what she was holding.

Maedeh texts me that she is doing "Göod"—I smile at the umlaut. She is ~~forgetting her Greek,~~ learning Swedish. She sends a picture of notebooks stacked on a window ledge and writes "For school." Sometimes there's a GIF in Greek, "TI KANEIS"; the first months in Sweden are in Porjus, a northern town covered in snow. It is November when I get a voice message from Saliha, Maedeh's mother. Her legs hurt in the cold, "very very pain," she writes, and "miss you very very." She didn't think to bring socks and tights ~~from Greece~~. There are no stores near where they are. "Cold very very," she writes under a picture of a snow-covered road and the boarding house where they are housed with other refugees.

Their last night in Athens, Maedeh walked to the top of the Lykabettus hill with Saliha and Mina to see the lights of the city, and "the beautiful Acropolis." Maedeh ~~had~~ smiled. "You had a party," I said. She shook her head, "~~No party~~ only dancing with music" back at the squat. "Everyone until late." Was that night ~~still~~ with her? As I ~~still~~ hear her voice and feel the muggy September air the afternoon I wept my goodbye, Maedeh surprised at my tears; ~~eleven when she arrived at the squat,~~ she was now thirteen. I'd brought my UGG boots to give her, thinking of the Swedish snow. Azize admired the brown suede. I gave Mina a black wool coat ~~I had no idea~~ my daughter would later ask for. The UGGs were in Azize's corner when I visited again, Maedeh's goodbye present, ~~left behind~~ for Azize.

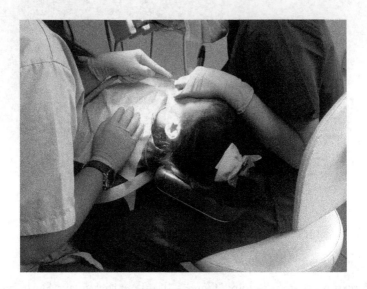

Mohammad Zia tells Eirini and I, ~~they've left for~~ ". . . Germany." Hennieh had another dentist appointment scheduled. "Azize sorry," he says. A man translates for Mohammad Zia that Azize ~~wanted to say goodbye but~~ had to leave when they got the chance. I give the things I had for Hennieh (leggings, a Minnie Mouse toothbrush, toothpaste). Mohammad Zia nods thank you. Eirini and I wander the dark camp and remember ~~a Christmas ago~~ when Hennieh and her friends, Hodah, Roshan, and Sahar, sang Greek kalanda songs running through puddles in the freezing night.

A message from Mohammad Zia says he would like to see me. He ~~wants something, or~~ is interested in meeting up? Azize, Hennieh, and Amir Houssein are ~~all gone,~~ now living outside of Frankfurt.

I meet Mohammad Zia and a friend of his at a café on Omonia Square. He is carrying a large gardenia plant full of budding flowers. I feel ashamed ~~of my suspicions~~. Mohammad Zia explains, as his friend translates, that he picked out the plant himself, that Azize wanted to thank me for helping with Hennieh's teeth. I buy coffee and orange juice and keep saying "thank you." He tells his friend to tell me God sent me ~~when they had nothing~~. I tell his friend to say God ~~had~~ sent us each other.

~~After months of no news,~~ I get a series of WhatsApp messages from Maedeh:

We live in GOTLAND
Haw is whit [How is with] Narghes?
Do you talk whit [with] her?
very could [cold]
I live on island
Last year we changed my house
We move to my brother
My address: Gotland

II

THE *RE* IN *REFUGE*

the opposite of nearness is not elsewhere but another figure of nearness
—Anne Dufourmantelle,
Of Hospitality: Anne Dufourmantelle Invites Jacques Derrida to Respond

The bus to the airport passed by the lower platia in Agia Paraskevi, my neighborhood. It was going to be a 4:30 a.m. flight to Geneva, the hour Maedeh left for Sweden, already two years ago. I am going to visit Narghes, her mother, grandmother, twin brother, and older brother, who received relocation papers in 2017. "Come, come . . ." she wrote on WhatsApp, and then in French, "Je voudrais bien te voir," after I'd said I wanted to see her. What had two years of being in Switzerland meant for Narghes and her family?

Kiosk vendors and drivers stopping for cigarettes seemed to be the only people awake. A cab driver pulls up to the kiosk, reeking of cigarettes, and buys three packs of Marlboros.

The airport bus is packed. A young mother covers her son's mouth and nose with a cloth mask (this is before COVID). He's half asleep as she loops the elastic behind each ear.

It's almost 5:30 when I check in, pausing at Accessorize where I would have picked up something for Hennieh. She was wearing the cat-shaped sunglasses I got her in one of the pictures Mohammed Zia sent from Germany over Messenger.

Narghes promised to be in Geneva when I arrived; we would go to Anières together, a town where her family was living in a compound of buildings; at the gates a sign will read: "Centre d'Anières, Aide aux migrants (AMIG)." But when I arrive at the Geneva airport, I don't see Narghes, and need to connect to the airport WiFi to call her; I have to add my ticket number or scanned boarding pass and can't find either.

What was it like for all five of them, especially for Fatima whose glaucoma-filmed eyes made it hard for her see, to arrive in this world? Malihé's aged mother, whom

Judi described as "ancient but probably isn't older than me," said little but always smiled. "When you embark on a journey, you have already arrived. The world you are going to is already in your head," Dionne Brand writes in *Map to the Door of No Return*. Tomorrow is a location. I'd like to know what someone like Mohammed does with his tomorrows; Mohammed who sent a pregnant Rakia to Germany with their three-year-old Asma, and who has so far not managed to move beyond his basement room at the Athens squat. Did being in Athens barricade his tomorrows? Were his todays less valuable without Rakia and Asma, even as he was tasked at the squat with managing its various crises like rationing water and arranging food deliveries? Mohammed showed us pictures of Asma in Germany, gap-toothed and now with shoulder-length hair. Narghes and Maedeh took turns running Asma in her stroller down the hallways; the corridors in winter were freezing and full of kids, and always draped with drying laundry. It was where Narghes slipped on a skateboard and chipped her front tooth. Kosta, the dentist who was doing pro bono work for the refugees, had fixed it for her; he did everything from fillings to root canals for two months of Sundays before his son was born.

Ibrahim, Narghes' older brother, calls. I can barely make out the words as he tells me to go to "La Garde," the Geneva train station where Narghes is waiting for me. "Avec le train," he says when I ask how to get there. The airport's spaciousness feels overwhelming. As I listen to the metallic rhythm of escalators, I wonder what I'll do if I don't find Narghes. The lit timetables and the floor's transparent shine amplify my anxiety. I remember Benjamin, a Swiss boyfriend who lived in Zurich that I had not thought of in years—would he be someone I'd be in touch with? Narghes sends a voice message with emojis and lines in French. There's a snapshot of escalators in front of a Coop shop, "Je suis ici," she writes. I answer, "Tu veux que je te trouve là bas?" And send a picture of where I am. I realize there are several Coop shops. I ask if she wants me to wait where I am. "Tu vas me trouver ici? A CHA-CHOU SHOP." Some forty minutes later I see a smiling Narghes walking towards me, a crate of strawberries under her arm, her chestnut-colored hair loose to her waist. We hug and laugh, and I tell her she is taller; "J'ai grossi," she says, telling me she's put on weight. I remind her of when she admired an actress at a play we went to in Athens and said she wanted to put on weight and look like her.

On the bus to Anières we share a sandwich I kept from the flight. I tell Narghes her hair looks thicker, and she tells me her eldest brother wanted her to keep it covered, that she never covers it now. I ask what her mother thinks; "Elle est d'accord," she says, meaning she agrees to let her have it uncovered. Then shows me the ends are split. We say we'll trim the lengths together. When we get off at a stop in the middle of a field, I see Unés waving to us from the other side of the road on a bicycle. We are surrounded by the Swiss countryside and wandering sheep. Carpets of yellow, maybe dandelion, break up lengths and lengths of green; we are very, very far from the Athens squat with its classrooms partitioned with hanging sheets.

The sign at the entrance of a building cluster reads: Centre d'Anières, Aide aux migrants (AMIG). Les ateliers d'Anières. Les fourneaux d'Anières. Lots of children are running around. People smile as we pass, many gathered on spread blankets and sheets in the open field. The buildings are surrounded by sheep farms. Narghes says, "Everyone happy," in English. It reminds me of the time I visited the Malakassa camp outside Athens and we had a picnic in the surrounding field. I wonder about the living spaces, and if bathrooms are communal. I see more children and families sitting on the grass, and notice a scent. The months of blocked drains and leaking porta-potties in the playground at the squat in Athens has triggered my sensitivity to smells.

In the entranceway, bouquets of dried flowers hang from the ceiling and a large *Welcome* on the wall greets us in languages that include French, Arabic, and English. Narghes ushers me through a hallway, the wall covered with images of children doing games and looking at us. "The road knows that wherever you find yourself you are," Dionne Brand writes, and Narghes points to her brother Unés smiling from one of the posters. It's a Christmas party and Unés is holding an elf doll. Colors from a stained-glass window in the stairwell throw rainbow colors over the steps; we walk through shades of orange and purple as we reach the third floor. Fatima, Narghes' grandmother, is waiting. Narghes laughs because as soon as she sees us, she disappears. Narghes tells me Fatima wanted to know which one I was of the various volunteers at the squat; she'd explained I was the one who took her to the dentist. Scattered shoes lay outside the rooms along the hallway. We take ours off at the door of A4.

Malihé is waiting. "Salām," I say, and we hug; "Salām, salām," she says, inviting me to sit. The room is small, neat, efficiently laid out. There's a couch against a wall on one side with a refrigerator next to it. A large plasma television sits on the floor. There's a table with two chairs, a rug over most of the floor, pillows, and a flat sponge mat where I sit down. Wooden steps at the end of the room lead to a bunk landing with a double mattress, mirror, and bureau, where Narghes and Malihé sleep. Unés sleeps on the couch. Fatima and Ibrahim have their own room next door. Fatima comes in and sits in a corner of the floor. The plasma is on an Afghan channel playing what looks like a burlesque, men with stuffed chests wearing wigs that fit badly are making exaggerated gestures that make Fatima laugh out loud. Malihé says something to Narghes who explains that they are "pas vraiment des femmes," not really women, and I nod, "Je sais ça." The television drowns out our bits of conversation. I'm suddenly exhausted. I ask Narghes if they have a bathroom and she says, "Pour tout le monde," meaning it's communal, past the kitchen that's also communal. Someone is cooking and I can smell fried garlic.

When I'm back in the room Narghes asks if the bathroom was okay; I nod, and try to explain that I didn't know how to flush. The toilets are squat toilets, what my father called "Turkish toilets," lined up in stalls. I forget to bring toilet paper with me. I use a plastic jug and fill it from the sink to pour water. Malihé understands, and ushers me to follow her back to the stalls where she shows me there's a lever to flush. She laughs at my expression of surprise when water gushes through a plastic tube.

We gather on the floor, as Narghes puts the strawberries she carried from Geneva into bowls. There's also cut up bananas and melon. Malihé takes out a jug of lassi from the refrigerator and the yogurt she's made; the lassi is rimmed with something dark; I think mold, but realize it's a spice, maybe cardamom, and it's delicious. There's steamed rice, spinach with garlic, chickpeas, and potatoes. I eat and eat. We are using forks and knives and spoons that we never used when we ate together at the squat; we scooped the food with bread and our fingertips. There's Malihé's flatbread, and now, also, cheese. When we're done Malihé gathers the plates and bowls and I pick up the empty pot of rice when she stops me. Narghes says, "Non, non, on fait pas ça chez nous!" Malihé tells her I'm a guest. "Don't do work," she says in English.

There are bowls of sweetened milk and a rice dessert Malihé takes from the refrigerator, but I've laid down against a pillow on the sponge mat and start to fall asleep. I feel a blanket laid over me. I hear Fatima's raucous laughter as she watches the Afghan channel. Narghes is on her cell phone and Malihé's on WhatsApp chatting with someone in Iran. There's a flash from Narghes' cellphone as she takes a picture of me almost asleep.

It's close to dawn when I wake up. I slip on one of the pairs of shoes outside the door and make my way to the toilets. This time I take a roll of paper towel with me. In the bathroom there's the scent again. I crush the roll to my nose. *First world*, I think to myself, *what if you had to do without for real?* Back in the room I notice Unés asleep on the couch, his glasses on the floor. Malihé and Narghes are still up in their bunk. On the floor cell phones are plugged into a power strip of sockets next to emptied shells of melon seeds. I imagine Narghes and Malihé eating the seeds while talking on their phones. I scoop up the shells. Malihé comes down the ladder and points to the bunk for me to use if I want to sleep some more. I gesture that I'm fine. "Chai?" she asks, pulling her scarf loosely over her head as she opens the window to fields of April's green.

Maybe this is the scent in the air, the yellow of dandelion, or onions? The brightness of the yellow reminds me of a Van Gogh painting. Malihé spreads the *souflan* mat on the floor. There is her flatbread and a baguette that she takes from a cloth bag hanging on a hook behind an open window. There is cheese again and more strawberries from the night before and the cut banana slices that now look bruised. Narghes comes down from the bunk and sits with us, we talk of taking the bus into Geneva. We will buy groceries for today's meal and visit the geyser on the lake. I realize that I'd forgotten to pack a towel. There were things I brought for the family, things they sometimes asked for while at the squat—hair dye for Malihé and Fatima, a black jean jacket for Narghes, T-shirts for Unés and Ibrahim. Though Malihé has let her hair go white, she nods when I give her the dye. "Swiss good?" I ask, spanning my hands around the room and toward the window. Fatima nods vigorously, putting her hand on her heart. Malihé says, "Iran, no," and Narghes explains. As asylum seekers, they must stay in Switzerland for five years before they can travel. Malihé is "Status F," the lowest, or the most basic, migrant category; possibilities for citizenship only come with "Status B."

An Afghan woman who lives in the next room knocks on the door and hands

Malihé a plate with a wedge of sweet bread she's made. I hear the word "Unan" re-peated, which is "Greece" in Farsi; Malihé lets her know this is where I have come from, that I helped get Narghes' tooth fixed. The Afghan woman had arrived with her youngest daughter from Crete, where her husband and other three daughters still are. I am guessing that she is in her twenties, but maybe she's younger. Malihé pours chai as they sit talking. Unés looks up from his cell phone with a smile and suddenly asks me how old I am. I'm not sure why I lie. I feel if I say fifty-seven it will surprise them, as I know Malihé looks older than she is, so I say, "Fifty," showing five sets of ten fingers. Malihé tells me I am young, "Tu es jeune," she says, and adds in Farsi, "I am younger, but I am old." Narghes translates. I tell Malihé she's had a hard life, and point to Narghes and Unés, say five children with my full hand of fingers. She nods. "Il m'a frappée," she says, and gestures with her fist against her head. I realize she is telling me her husband was part of what made life difficult, that he hit her. I know she was married at twelve, because Ibrahim told me, but hearing it from her makes the fact of it newly chilling. "C'est pas bien," I say, it's not good, and Malihé nods agreement, "Non, pas bien." She shows me the same picture she'd shown me in Athens, her child self with makeup, a bride, then tells me she is forty-three. "J'ai quarante-trois ans. Mais je suis vieille." I try to say I would be old or "vieille" too if I had had her life. "Tu es mariée?" she asks. I say I am not married, to which she says "InshaAllah," God willing, then, "moi, non," to emphasize that she doesn't want another husband.

We take the bus from Anières to the "Plage Genève" stop. Narghes and Unés want me to walk under the geyser. I take pictures. Narghes also wants us to take the boat to the other side of the lake. I'd like to walk some more, though this is more of a pastime for me than for her and Unés. She ushers me away from certain streets, explaining they are the ones with expensive shops; we pass a yogurt stall where we get extravagant, colored combinations. Unés wants his with chocolate chip sprin-kles and M&Ms. We go into a pharmacy for something to treat Narghes' acne and buy Avène liquid soap. We walk into a C&W department store. Narghes spots a yellow spaghetti-strapped dress and I suggest she try it on. I try on a bathing suit and stare at my middle-aged body. My stomach no longer flat, my thighs and upper arms loose. But it is my skin and body; like the smell that seeped from the toilets in the building it fills me with a vague revulsion; the body that pees and hurts, eats and ages, still dreams and is conduit to *the world you are going to . . . already in your head*. It would be too simple to say I didn't like what I saw, or what I smelled; what I saw and smelled skewed a construction of reality *already in* [my] *head*. I needed to better trust where the road was taking me, remember Brand's, *The road knows that wherever you find yourself you are*.

Narghes tells me she will not take the yellow dress that looks "terrible" on her, and I tell her I won't get the bathing suit either. Outside of the dressing rooms we find Unés who hands me a black T-shirt on a hanger and a black baseball cap. "Tu veux ça?" I ask. He smiles sheepishly. Narghes takes the shirt from him when I say I'll get it for him. We head to the boat and cross the lake. It's warm and Unés is tired. Once we get to the other side Unés takes off his socks and shoes and puts his feet into the water. Three swans approach us; they keep plunging their gorgeous necks into the water then pull them out, fluttering their feathers. Their beaks glisten. I ask Narghes what kinds of shops are on this side of the lake, she says she doesn't know. We walk to a pebble beach where a swan sits on a matting of twigs and brush. Two boys hang over the guardrail teasing her. I almost say something, but they move on.

The swan is magnificent. Her neck turns as she occasionally gazes at us with large charcoal-rimmed eyes. The last time I was in Geneva, I was visiting Benjamin, and saw the city through his eyes, the world of a professor with various happy advantages. On the pier with Unés and Narghes I was experiencing a different city. We didn't go into cafés, certainly no restaurants, though we passed plenty of people sitting in both. I'd been warned of how expensive even a cup of tea could be. We had more in common with the swan, exposed as she was to passersby, the lake and city, everything as tangible as the quay's warm concrete. Narghes said they had visited the area at Christmas with her older brother, Malihé, and Fatima, "C'était très joli," she says, describing how pretty the lighted streets were and how music played the entire time.

In a Coop we run into Malihé and Fatima. Malihé's bright red scarf covers her hair, and Fatima's glaucoma-filmed eyes are kohl-rimmed. They look happy, wandering the city with a shopping cart now filled with groceries. We greet each other with the gestures and repeated words we used in Athens, and now in this Swiss capital where Malihé and her family have found refuge—"The *re-* in *refuge* means basically 'back' or 'backward' rather than 'again'" (*Merriam-Webster*). I was here because I was looking back to a place and time we had shared in Athens, one that had brought them, and us, to this day on a map of various tomorrows. It felt as if we had never stopped greeting each other.

At the Anières apartments, I ask Narghes which stall to use in the communal bathroom to take a shower. In the largest stall she puts a plastic chip against the faucet to show me how to keep the water running as they automatically shut off to conserve water. The vague scent of the toilets lingers as I quickly soap, wash, and rinse myself. I'm back in their apartment, toweled and dressed, when Malihé and Narghes look surprised. "You finish?" Narghes asks. I explain that the plastic chip kept slipping and the water didn't run continuously. Malihé wants to show me how to place the chip more firmly, the way she showed me where the toilet lever was. She tells me I can now shower, but I say I'm done, and remember the trip to Rhodes when Judi and I took Narghes, Unés, Maedeh, and Amir Hussein on a retreat during the Greek Easter break. Narghes, thirteen at the time, had been impressed that we washed the dishes so quickly. "We clean *very very*," she had said, showing me that sponging the plates and pans involved a lot of soap and scrubbing. I'd written down the remark along with the fact that the German volunteers who arrived from Hamburg had kept their watches on German time throughout their stay.

When it's Narghes' turn, she spends close to an hour in the shower. We're going to trim her hair. We bought a hair mask, but she forgets to take it into the shower. When she's back in the room, her hair is bunched in knots. The supermarket-bought shampoo is probably full of chemicals; I say, "C'est pas bon, ça." I spread the mask into her hair and Narghes smiles at how easily the comb's teeth glide through the tangled strands. Malihé is again talking on the phone to someone in Iran. Later I ask about Malihé's sister who had come with us on the picnic in Malakassa. Elias, her nine-year-old son, had cried when we didn't take him to Rhodes with us. Malihé shakes her head and gestures. Her sister is now in Germany; two sons are in Austria, a daughter is in Germany, another in Canada; Elias is in Greece with his father. "Pas bien," she tells me, shaking her head that it's not good that everyone is in different parts of the world.

I glimpse a woman and a man with a child on Malihé's cell phone. She shows them who I am through the WhatsApp video cam, then goes back to the conversation. That Malihé is now in Switzerland instead of Greece is little consolation as her loved ones in Iran are her measure of geography. When she's off the phone she explains, as Narghes translates, that it wasn't always expensive to cross into Europe. That people, like her eldest son, walked. He was sixteen. Every year, she says it gets harder, and more expensive. Last year smugglers were taking 4,000 to 4,500 euros per person; now it's 5,000. Fatima has been watching another burlesque on the Afghan channel, and suddenly smiles at me. I gesture to her that it is nice to be here. Fatima gives me a wide toothless grin, her wrinkles deep as gashes, but her feet, their delicacy and skin, are youthful. Narghes touches the trimmed ends of her hair to her cheeks and tells me they are soft, "Mes cheveux sont très doux." I pick up the packet of hair mask to say it's all thanks to this, "C'est tout ça!"

Malihé wants to know if I'd like something to eat. "J'ai toujours faim," she says, slicing an apple. I'm not hungry, and tell her I'll wait for lunch. She is often with a bowl of nuts and raisins, a plate of cut fruit. As with so many of the women I met at the squat, never far from children, I wonder if this constant giving isn't what makes Malihé hungry for something that will feed her too. In the days I am at Anières, Malihé is always doing something, folding clothes, sheets, or blankets, preparing a meal, on WhatsApp talking to someone in Iran. Now she scrolls through her phone to show me pictures. There's a man dressed in black, bearded, wearing leather boots, leaning against a car. He looks like he could be a soldier, tall, heavy-set; this was my husband, she says. I ask how old he was when they married; she says twenty-six. He had wanted a lot of children. "Toujours," Malihé says, this time referring to her childbearing body. But I think she repeats "toujours" with some bewilderment, as the child who was forced to provide "toujours," *always*, for a growing family when she was a child herself.

In one photograph Malihé is seventeen, in another twenty-nine, in another thirty-five; she is very specific about the ages, showing me the different expressions on her face, the styles of dress; sometimes she is without a hijab so I can see her hair cut in a bob. "Pas bien," she repeats, as in not well, of a photograph of her newly married child self. I nod. She then shows me a picture of an attractive woman who wanted to marry her eldest son, and shakes her head, letting me know she didn't accept her as a daughter-in-law. I learn it's a tradition in the culture, the approval of a daughter-in-law by the groom's mother. There is something shrewd about an arrangement in which a mother would have to approve the woman her son chooses to marry; in an economy that upholds gendered parameters and roles, it gives her a power. Another picture on her phone is of a girl who died. She was twenty-nine, "très belle," a pretty woman. She gets up from the floor to get another bowl of fruit from the refrigerator. Would I prefer pears to the apples she sliced? Again, I say no, but feel Malihé is hurt that I don't share her appetite, and say, "Oui, merci."

The day before I leave Narghes and I take the bus back into Geneva. I tell her I'd like to go to the place she'd shown me on a WhatsApp video. Fatima and Malihé were dancing to a song in Farsi with the backdrop of the Alps; it was not a scene from *The Sound of Music* but it reminds me of *The Sound of Music*. We decide to go there after Geneva where Narghes wants to buy makeup, but first we walk through the botanical gardens with its lush trees and various stone fountains. There are water taps with signs noting, "eau potable." Narghes delights in drinking from them. I remember the guide in Pompeii telling us how drinking water was available everywhere in that city too. These days companies like Nestlé are bottling once freely available water to sell for profit. Perhaps the measure of a civilization lies in the extent to which it respects its citizens' basic needs, from water to health care. "C'est tout propre ici," I say to Narghes about how orderly everything looks. There are clearly marked public toilets, bus schedules posted at kiosks as well as bus stops, recycling bins outside shops and cafés.

In the department store Narghes lingers over the foundations and mascaras. She says they don't allow mascara at school, but she likes to wear it, and tries it on, standing in front of a small mirror. A handsome saleswoman at the Guerlain counter says she has just the creams for Narghes' acne; she wants to give her a makeover if we have a little time. Narghes nods, smiling as she seats herself in the makeup chair. The saleswoman pulls Narghes' hair away from her face and pats her cheeks and forehead with pads dipped in lotion. Tubes of cream come out of a stylish kit. I'm absorbed in the deft application of assorted products as Narghes lets her skin be covered with dabs of a thin-haired brush. The handsome saleswoman is telling us how good all of this is for her face, that Narghes' skin is so much like mine. We laugh at her assumption that we are mother and daughter. Narghes is enjoying the attention and her skin begins to glow, the acne calmed and camouflaged. I think we might buy the tube of cream and say so to the saleswoman who produces a second tube, saying they go together: the one a therapy, the other a foundation. We follow her to another counter to see exactly what this amounts to. Narghes is happy with her face but takes a deep intake of breath when she hears the price. She tells me there is no need to buy anything. I'm thinking I would like to please her, convinced the acne cream is good. The saleswoman tells us that all Guerlain products are made of natural extracts. I manage to say they are also expensive. I toy with getting one tube. It's tiny and Narghes is visibly anxious that I might buy it. Narghes and I would like to discuss this further, I tell the saleswoman, who looks disappointed. She lets us know that she's always at the Guerlain counter and would be happy to help at any point. As we push through the revolving doors, Narghes lets out a loud sigh. I tell her that if she had really wanted the cream, I could have bought it for her. "C'est très peu ça pour l'argent," she says, meaning we would be getting very little for our money. When we are back on the streets, Narghes lets me know that she doesn't go into department stores because Malihé says if they don't have the money to spend, they shouldn't be in them. I nod, and say sometimes when we see things, we get ideas. She also tells me that one day she'd like to be a translator or lawyer, or work in a bank.

The sky is dark with rain clouds as we head to the lakefront. We take two buses then walk through an upscale neighborhood with blooming islands of tulips in the middle of the road. Trees loom over high garden walls. Once at the lake Narghes walks to the end of the pier, spreading her arms to the sky. It starts to rain, and I want to leave. "Pourquoi?" she asks. "C'est très beau ici!" A full storm is about to break. I insist we make our way back. We walk at a clip along the open fields with their bands of dandelion-yellows, past the perfectly kept tulips, pausing at a bus stop as we decide it would be faster to walk since the next bus isn't for another twenty minutes. The sky splits open and the downpour begins in earnest. Narghes is smiling. I smile back, but anxiously. There's thunder and the fields grow dark. Lightning and more thunder continue as we jog the last stretch toward Les Ateliers, soaked. Unés is in the entranceway with a young boy who looks about ten or twelve and waves at us. Narghes tells me it's always the young kids that ask to play with Unés.

Malihé laughs as we walk in drenched. The woman from Afghanistan whose husband is in Crete is there too. She knows I'm leaving the next day. Ibrahim is unpacking a bag of food from the store where the Atelier residents get weekly supplies with their coupons. He tells me that the Afghan woman wants to know if I can help her find a Greek lawyer for her husband. He makes the overnight boat trip to Athens from Crete every week and is told at the asylum offices that his turn has not come up yet; they keep telling him to come back, and he keeps being turned back. Malihé has cooked chickpeas and spinach and chopped onions, tomatoes, and cucumbers into a salad. Everyone's hungry. Narghes eats from the edge of a serving platter, Unés from the pot. Malihé says the rice isn't good because the oil is burnt. I say it's delicious, which it is. Again, Malihé refuses to let me gather the plates. I go to brush my teeth, and when I'm back in the room Unés is smiling as he hands me a gift wrapped in paper. Narghes is smiling too. Unés tells me it is for me to open when I'm back in Athens. I say they didn't have to give me anything when Narghes says I'll like it.

The Afghan woman has left and returned, and again there's cake on a plate which she offers us. I ask her how she came to be in Switzerland. She says she was told it was a good country to live in, that she was looking for a country that would be safe and asked people. I'm struck by the naïveté of her statement, as much as its common sense. She needs to find a Greek lawyer who can speak to her Swiss lawyer. The Swiss lawyer is apparently optimistic but needs to talk to someone in Greece. I know as much to say that if her husband has filed for asylum in Greece, it would be impossible to file elsewhere. No, he had not; he's waiting to find a way to join her in Switzerland with their children. Malihé is on her phone again with someone in Iran. After she hangs up, she says something happened. Ibrahim translates. A couple had left their sleeping child in the car as they were unpacking it when someone stole the car with the baby in it. Malihé is talking in rapid Farsi, clearly upset. "They forgot the baby?" I say in English. Malihé nods. "How old was it?" I ask Ibrahim. Malihé says two, a girl.

The Afghan woman says something to Malihé, then asks Ibrahim if I've understood her request. I tell him to tell her I'll ask about a lawyer in Athens. I get her husband's cell phone number and name. I suggest he could stay at the squat instead of going back and forth to Crete. She thanks me, *tashakor*, she says, and *merci*, and then offers me cake, but I've brushed my teeth, and thank her. She smiles and takes a slice. "She's not like us," Malihé says in Farsi, "hungry all the time." Ibrahim translates this with a short laugh. "Merci beaucoup," I tell her. "De rien," Malihé answers.

The sky is still dark when Malihé comes down from the bunk. She wants to make chai, but I tell her there's no need. There is cheese in the refrigerator she asks me to take with me. I go up to the bunk where Narghes is sleeping. She wanted to come to the airport and told me to wake her but she's sound asleep. Ibrahim offers to get me as far as the airport bus that leaves from Geneva. I kiss Narghes' cheek, and say, "Au revoir, Narghes; on se parlera quand je serai arrivée en Grèce," telling her I'll call from Athens. She murmurs something without waking. I'm anxious about getting the bus and climb down to see Ibrahim in the doorway with his backpack on his shoulder, waiting. I laugh at how awake he looks. He tells me he's been up, and can't sleep when he has something to do. Malihé and I hug in the doorway, "Tu vas revenir?" She asks if I'll return, and I nod, "Oui, merci," and again she says, "De rien," and again we hug. Ibrahim insists on carrying my bag as we walk down the stairwell. The sky is streaked in shades of indigo. Dawn light glazes the mountain peaks. The sheep are huddled in their shed as we walk toward the bus stop. Ibrahim tells me of a friend who killed himself "because of a girl," he says in English. The girl had left him after a year together. "He was my friend," Ibrahim says almost flatly, and then repeats the fact and says, "Yes," when I ask if he was a good friend. He tells me he cried a lot. "It's not worth it for a girl," he says in English, and then in French, "C'est pas grave, non? Pour une bonne amie," noting that it was unnecessary, he doesn't understand why anyone would kill themselves for a lover. I ask if he had any family. Ibrahim says they were in Iran; his friend had his papers and was going to bring one of his brothers over. "Now, nothing," he says, and shakes his head.

We are the only ones at the stop when the bus pulls up. I don't have the exact change, and the machine isn't working. Ibrahim has a pass. The driver says, "C'est pas grave," and lets me ride without a ticket. We get to Geneva and switch to the airport bus. Ibrahim comes with me. I'm happy he's decided to come to the airport. He says he takes a bicycle from Anières all the way to Rive, "le vélo jusqu'à Rive." Sometimes he has so much energy that he bikes the distance. He's done it several times, met up with pals. They have a drink, then he bikes back. A sign for a watch repair shop, "Master of Complications," catches my eye from the bus window. Ibrahim describes the family's arrival in Switzerland, the five of them with all their bags on a bus. People stared. He laughs, "It's nothing now to go around," he says in English, "but then I was afraid, once really afraid." After a soccer match someone pushed back his shoulder. "Like that," he shows me, abruptly jerking his shoulder backward. I nod. "Like the Golden Dawn in Greece," he says, referring to the fascist party that had won Parliament seats in the elections that brought the Greek

Syriza government to power. "Now I fight," he says lightly. The family had mistakenly ended up on the Italian border when a policeman looked at their papers and brought them to Anières. I ask if he'll stay for a coffee when we get to the airport. "D'accord," he says and nods. This is the first time I order a café au lait and realize I've wanted to order one for days. "Café au lait et une petite tarte aux framboises," I say to the young man behind the counter. I'm pleased with the sound of my French. I've missed the language. Ibrahim orders "un chocolat avec un croissant." He wants to show me pictures on his cell phone of a school excursion to a chalet. He's with a group of classmates on their winter break; they look like they're having a great time. "We snuck in some vodka," he says. "It must have warmed you up. Il fait froid en hiver." He agrees, "Bien oui," and shows me a picture of himself he's proud of: skiing down a mountain slope looking agile and expert.

Unés' gift is a cloth bag he sewed that opens and closes with a pulled cord. The fabric is light blue with tiny white hearts. Unés had gone with Fatima for a free sewing lesson the day before I left. He said his favorite thing to do was to make bags. There's also a WhatsApp message from Narghes saying she's sorry she missed me. Then I get a row of weeping emojis. Her cousin Elias was taken off a plane in a country he doesn't know; Malihé's sister had made it to Germany and found a way to send for her son. I remember Elias' expression when we didn't take him with us on the trip to Rhodes.

After several frantic messages over WhatsApp, Narghes says the authorities put Elias on a plane to Germany from Austria. For my part, I called a lawyer whose name I found from Judi. When I tell the lawyer about the Afghan woman with her husband in Crete, she's warm. She will get in touch with the woman's husband tomorrow. "Me to kaló (*με το καλό*)," I say, "with the good," a Greek expression; it gives tomorrow a shape.

"PSYHI MOU"

. . . to feel at home nowhere, but at ease almost everywhere.
—Georges Perec

You need to be able to receive beauty.
—Katerina Iliopoulou

I

I am on the island of Patmos for Easter. Though I haven't come for the holiday specifically. It so happens I'm off from work because it's Easter, arguably the most important event in the Greek holiday calendar; Christ's birth the less celebrated event as compared to his death as a necessary prelude to resurrection. Patmos, the island where St. John the Divine is said to have had his vision of the apocalypse, generally feels mournful this time of year. Not infrequently it will be a sun-splashed day anywhere else in Greece while here clouds gather in their overcast grays. I am not a believer, though I'm hard put to call myself an atheist. Perhaps agnostic, with its Greek root, is closest to describing my feeling—that is, *gnōsis* (knowledge), and so *agnōsto* (unknown) would make me a believer in the unknown.

It is always night when I arrive. The ferries leave Piraeus in the late afternoon or early evening and make several ports of call before arriving at Patmos. When I get off the boat in the small island harbor, the dark is full of scents and the whitewash glows.

The winter's cold was still palpable when I entered the house. I visit irregularly because it takes anywhere from eight to twelve hours by boat to reach, yet its distance from my life in Athens was one of the reasons I bought the house. A year ago I had come with my then-relationship and his son. I wondered whether the visit had been part of why he had not ended the relationship earlier. That he wanted his son to have the gift of the island. "Gifts," my friend A would say months later, "are never innocent." A was referring to the chocolate bars I had bought for his son after we were no longer involved. I was defensive, then a little angry at A's comment; I had bought the chocolate for the boy who I knew liked a particular Greek brand, and given it in the spirit of a bond I felt still important. After all, I said to A, our lives are too full of ruptures.

That first night, the house held me with its traces of conversation, meals, moments, and hours of love. *Held*, I think, rather than *housed*, as I now take in the damp wood tang, notice rust streaks on the wall in the kitchen bled from one of the latches on the window. There are always repairs that need attending to when I visit: more whitewashing, the cutting back of jasmine and the lemon tree branches, following the tiny dust lines to where termites have burrowed their way into a shutter or wood cupboard. I am indebted to those from the island who have helped me, sometimes very generously, sometimes waiting for months to be paid for work that has helped me hold the house together.

Xristodolos, a man whose earnestness is so out of sync with the times, will offer to fix a shutter, or a lock, saying, "Let me do it," as if the possibility of my refusing his offer would cause more damage than leaving the lock unfixed or the shutter unpainted. He once said he didn't know why he did the unpaid repairs, but that it made him happy. Xristodolos is a carpenter, and he paints the wood he turns into doors and shutters and cabinets, but he also took the time to explain to me how to run the toilet's underground piping so it didn't obstruct the roots of the lemon trees. He often reminds me of things I've since forgotten, such as the time he showed me how someone had laid their brick in a way that would make it less costly for me when I was fixing the house.

Then there's Maria, who I pay to look in on the house when I'm not there, who makes the soft *mizithra* cheese and has chickens, who always brings a bag of eggs with her when she comes to see me or comes to be paid. In 2014 I was especially low on cash and apologized for not being able to give her more money. "*Psyhi mou*," she said and nodded, though not without disappointment. *Psyhi mou* translates as "my soul." She was telling me she would not let me go, even if I couldn't give her the money I owed her, that she would continue to water the potted plants and the two lemon trees, to check on the house after a hard rain or windstorm.

I'd recently come across Genese Grill's essay, "Portals: Cabinets of Curiosity, Reliquaries and Colonialism," which describes, among other things, her time in the Loire Valley of France, in a house built by her hostess's grandfather, a carpenter.

Grill's admiration for the uninterrupted continuities of lives tied to place speaks to what I love about Patmos and its village community. Grill writes, "Every material thing here is bound or connected to the past via bloodlines, via deep ruts in the fields, etchings on the surface of earth's memory that reach deep down under the soil to places we cannot see but surely feel." She explains how such bonds engender a respect for "the mana of objects," a phrase she quotes from the French sociologist Marcel Mauss's 1954 study, *The Gift*, which explores the reasons for and forms of ancient economies of gift exchange. Grill borrows the term to foreground the layers of history objects can carry. She describes "the sense we have of powers inherent in old things and old places," how these traces are severed when objects, and people too, are commoditized and turned into "a mere thing." So when Maria says, *"psyhi mou,"* she reminds me that I am not a mere thing, or a mere wallet.

This house is its own portal into past histories, as is the island. There are the island's ties to the disappearing art of stone masonry, which lives on in a handful of the men who have passed it on to a handful of sons. There is the cave where St. John had his vision, that literal portal at the bottom of a rock enclave where a hole in the stone is rimmed in silver to show how he grabbed the ledge to raise his aged body and speak his apocalypse to Prokopis, his scribe. The house's portal is one of connections: to those who have shared it with me, helped make it habitable those first years I owned it, who have stayed here with me, and those who continue to help me care for it. These past histories bring on deep dream states, and the night I arrived in Patmos, I woke frightened. I'd had a nightmare in which a boy was threatened, a hot iron being pressed against his face, and I was cupping handfuls of water over his eyes, splashing them incessantly and asking if he felt pain. The boy shook his head and told me he felt nothing. Gaston Bachelard says that if he were "asked to name the chief benefit of the house" it would be that it "shelters daydreaming" and "protects the dreamer." In the middle of the night, I got up and walked down the narrow wooden steps to the bathroom, sweat gluing my skin despite the cold, feeling unprotected, if held, in the darkness.

All week, Holy Week for those who believe, people wish each other *"Kali Anastasi"* ("Good Resurrection"), the wish expressed with the same well-intentioned familiarity as "good morning" or "goodnight." Despite the fact that I have no Orthodox leanings, I am comforted by the words. They assume a connection of goodwill I don't always feel but always appreciate. It's like Maria speaking to me of the house's cracked shutters and sun-eaten pillows as if they were hers, the way Xristodolos says, "Μη μου στεναχωριεσαι" (*Me mou stenahoreisai*), when I tell him it might be another year or two before I can do anything to fix the wood shutters and doors. The phrase translates as "Don't worry yourself for me," and syntactically suggests that my upset will upset the person speaking to me. It makes my worry etymologically symbiotic—another word whose Greek roots σύν (with) + βίωσις (living) situate my worry in Xristodolos's and indebts me to him.

Indebtedness is also what Genese Grill discusses when she writes of how our commoditized worlds have given us a "freedom from the group" and its collective ties to ritual and obligation. I think of Maria and Xristodolos, whose help and care for the house is offered in sometimes unpredictable ways. I could have said less conventional, but conventional would suggest more of an obligation; their help is so often an offering, more of *psyhi* or soul than any sense of duty. Xristodolos surprises me with extra shelves in the bathroom and tells me that he thought they would be useful but does not want money for them. He is teaching me of a debt to the work of rootedness rather than to the roots themselves, of what it means to belong to more than what we might own, helping me to connect to people like him who have helped me care for the house. Maybe this is one of the ways gifts can become an overture of *con*ciliation—not necessarily *re*conciliation—connecting bodies that might otherwise remain estranged. When Maria says to me over the phone, "Your pillows are all eaten up by the sun. You have to get new ones," I surprise myself with the single-mindedness with which I go hunting for pillows to send to her from Athens, feeling as if not doing so would be showing her that I didn't share her urgency to protect the house from time's encroachments.

Giannis, a carpenter, is another person who helps me care for the house. He warns me that what I bring into it might be a danger, and he means the warped pieces of driftwood I collect. He says, "You'll infest your floorboards and the rest of the wood." I imagine tiny weevils burrowing into solid beams, what was once a ship's mast that runs across the ceiling of this century-old house. I wonder if my impulse to collect these pieces of nature isn't reflective of a primitive instinct, a kind of homage to forces with the power to transform and destroy, the way animals will sniff out the bones of dead prey—some reminder of the force, or animal, that reduced a once-living creature to bones.

I have rocks from the island's various beaches all over the house, on window ledges, my nightstand, in a soap dish, ashtray. Most of them are from Lampi, the beach of beautiful but gradually disappearing gem-colored rocks of browns and greens and purple reds. People like me have not been able to resist taking a few at a time, though some leave with boxfuls. When I gather these rocks and pieces of driftwood, I think of them as talismanic emblems of the larger natures that made them. I wonder too if that makes me any different from someone like Lord Elgin, who cut away at the Parthenon to ship friezes back to England, who could not stop cutting away once he got started—both of us consumed with beauty we want to possess.

I love the weight of the Lampi rocks in my palms, their surfaces smooth as skin, and the sound of them in the rolling surf, that the water and light perform a magic of their painterly collages. When my lover visited, we picked some rocks from the beach and he carted them back to the US, where he put them in a bowl of water in his house so their shine would keep something of that summer. Maybe he too wanted to take something of the island with him. I should have known that the relationship was over when I visited him a year later and the bowl had been emptied.

Markos, a gardener who sells plants on the island, furrows the soil with his rough hands to show me how to plant the basil I've bought from him. He cradles the roots gently, shaking them out from their plastic cup as he plants the tendrils. He tells me the soil in the pots—this dirt I'd brought with me from Athens because it was cheaper—is too full of what look like tiny Styrofoam pebbles. "Business," he says in English, making the word sound newly bitter. He smirks, tells me I should know better than not to trust him and his dirt. He points to the pine tree from my neighbor's garden looming over my two lemon trees and tells me it's foreign. "We had nothing on the island but our trees," by which he means the lemons, figs, and olives. Not the imported pines, or the palms that brought with them "the worm." Then he tells me matter-of-factly that he could "get rid of" the tree. I look at him as he offers to kill the looming pine if I'm willing to buy the poison. I laugh despite myself. He nods seriously and assures me he could do it easily. I say we aren't going to poison anything, and that I'll ask my neighbor Eleni if she could trim down its rising ferny tip. He shakes his head, and says she's also foreign, "ξένη" ("xeni")— that she isn't from the island and is wealthy. I remind him I'm not from the island either. He shakes his head again and says, "πονάς το νησί" ("you pain for the island"), using this familiar vernacular as opposed to the more grammatical and formal, "πονάτε το νησί" ("you feel the pain of the island"). This would more clearly, and grammatically, separate me from the island, whereas in Markos' rendering, the island and I have become one and the same, much in the way that Xristodolos tells me that my worry becomes his.

In the port, someone calls out, "*Ach ti myrodithies!*" ("What scents!"). This morning before Easter Sunday, the aromas of freshly baked sweet bread and raisin pastries waft through the streets. The children look especially well dressed, girls in colored tights with bows and barrettes in their hair, the boys in starched shirts. The scene makes me think of a Georges Perec passage from "The World"; not interested in "the grandiose" or "the impressive" or "even the foreign," he wants to experience the "familiar rediscovered." Is that why Maria looks so defeated when she says she receives "not even a thank you" for all she does in her family, for the houses she takes care of? She is continually offering, and her world continually takes her offerings for granted, failing to see the worth in her familiar acts. She is unappreciated, she says: the sheets she washes and irons, the eggs and cheese she brings to people, are not received as the gifts they are. When she comes over, we chat and fold sheets together. I never fold sheets in Athens, at least not very carefully, nor do I think of replacing the old apartment door or repairing the apartment windows that need screens and new handles. But here, in my house on Patmos, Maria insists we fold the sheets after I've hung them to dry. And as we fold, I listen to her telling me that her brother hung himself last summer, that her Good Friday was black because she remembers last year—"A whole man gone," saying, "If he had only talked to me." Her chest heaves like the sea and we hug, buoyed by some part of each other we are holding onto.

It's Maria I think of when I see the burst latch on the kitchen door and the hole in a window frame that looks gnawed. I put "putty" on my list of things to get from the store in the village. It's Maria who understands time will ravage the best of intentions and that that which is within our reach is only so ephemerally.

In the kitchen, where I'm writing, there is a large silkscreen of pastel-colored cherubs on the wall, *The Dawn of Love* written in an ornate cursive beneath the winged figures. The print, framed in its gold-leafed wood, hung in my great-grandfather's house in Patras, a port town in the Peloponnese. A Nazi bullet had pierced the bottom part of the frame during the Occupation. As my great aunt tells it, she'd been tending to her bedridden mother when the stray, or perhaps not so stray, bullet came into the living room from the street, and the bottom part of *The Dawn of Love* "τραυματίστηκε" ("was traumatized"), she liked to say. My great-grandfather took the print and other furniture when the family left the Prince Islands during Atatürk's purging of the Greeks after the 1922 "Smyrna Catastrophe," as the Greeks name it. Another portal of history, one that was awkward and burdensome to carry.

Genese Grill says "everything is a bearer of history" and describes the fact that the more objects circulate "the more mana they accumulate," which means *The Dawn of Love* carries at least a world war's worth of mana, and trauma too. This print was left hanging in the apartment where my great-grandmother and great-aunt had died, in a home whose unpatched ceiling let in the sky. I brought it to this house because the bullet hole reminded me that love's airy cherubs were not without damage.

Lewis Hyde's relatively more recent, and much-referenced, study on gift economies, *The Gift: Imagination and the Erotic Life of Property* (1983), makes a key distinction between "worth" and "value" to distinguish a gift from a commodity. To Hyde, worth refers to things we prize but cannot assign a price to. Value, in contrast, is part of a marketable exchange. "A gift has worth." Once the gift is given an exchange value, it ceases being a gift. For Hyde, gifts have the ability to transform the nature of those involved; he calls this *eros*-trade. He distinguishes this from *logos*-trade, which "draws the boundary" and keeps the exchange transactional, as in two people, or two countries, unmoved or untouched, by what passes between them. *Eros*, Hyde says, "obliterates" boundaries in its overture to the other that also risks rejection. This was probably why A criticized the chocolates I gave to my no-longer lover's son. I'd wanted to obliterate the boundary that the breakup had created: to let the boy know that the breakup wasn't the only thing I remembered, to placate something of the violence of the fact of it so that something of that loss might return to me something of myself.

"*Xristos Anesti!*" ("Christ is Resurrected!") people declare as church bells toll those first minutes of Easter Sunday. Lit tapers bloom in the dark, spreading candlelight; they let us know the mourning is over, that a body's frailties have given over to its soul, and the darkness was not meant to last. On "New Tuesday"—Νέα Τρίτη (Nea Triti)—icons are unhoused, carried out of churches and monasteries and walked through the island streets. Cafés and shops keep their doors open as they pass. Giannis sees me in the square and says, "It's been years, where have you been?" even though we had seen each other a summer ago. I say I've been here all week and ask about the saints the icons represent. He tells me they're the martyrs "burned, hung, tortured" for a better good. These saints with their suppliant lives, their private wagers with the godhead, are more real to me than today's very public assurances of "*Xristos Anesti!*" Someone passes and says, "*Alithos O Kyrios*" ("He is truly [risen]"). I mumble, "*alithos,*" which translates as "really" as much as "truly," and do not mention the Lord. And yes, this moment that celebrates what continues in memory and words is against *lithi*, meaning "forgetfulness," which must be, too, where the river Lethe gets her name. One of the five rivers in Hades' mythic underworld, Lethe flows through the cave of Hypnos (the god of sleep), bordering Elysium, the paradise where only heroes and those related to the gods can enter. *Alithia* (truth), then, is *lithi*'s antidote. Etymologically too, α-λήθεια, or *a-lithia* ("against forgetfulness"), is the salvage of light from oblivion's darkness. So I listen to the sounds that connect me to something of the centuries of ritual, and when another person passes and repeats, "*Xristos Anesti!*" I say again, "*alithos.*"

II

I have returned to Athens where I wake in my apartment remembering the island and am full of melancholy. I call Maria and before she says anything about the house, she says, "You forgot the cheese." She had told me to take it, and is hurt to find the *mizithra* still in the freezer. "Remember me when you eat it," she'd said, and meant, remember the days on the island—that she was there, is still there, while I am away. Remember we folded sheets and she wept speaking of her brother, that people including his wife and children seem to have forgotten him. More than anything, remember her pain, and that it would be months before we would see each other again. "I like to work in the houses," Maria had said about the coming summer, sweat shining on her cheeks and forehead. The work helped her forget the winter with its island winds howling through the empty alleyways and the stray cats looking for food.

I had forgotten Maria's gift and, as we spoke, was mortified that I'd done what her family and others had done in repeatedly taking her for granted. "Gratitude," Hyde says, "requires an *unpaid* debt." Bonds established between the one who offers and the one who receives a gift are severed when it fails to inspire gratitude, or in Hyde's words, when that "*unpaid* debt" is not "*felt.*" I tried to assure Maria I had truly forgotten the cheese in my rush to get myself onto the boat back to Athens, that I was grateful for it but, yes, had not remembered to take it. "*Nai, psyhi mou,*" ("Yes, *psyhi mou*") she said, assuring me again that she was still there.

It's several months before I'm back on the island. I'm watching the cats in the courtyard, especially the black one I'd called Pirate until I heard the Italians renting the neighbor's house call her Nero, and realized he was a she. My own cat is curious. She sidles up when I pet Nero, hissing as Nero gets close. Hurricane Harvey has been in Facebook updates all week. Friends and friends of friends are posting love and support. I'd told myself I would stay away from social media while on the island, then feel somehow negligent of the world when I log on in spite of myself and see the news. There are images of floating cars, descriptions of people climbing up flights of stairs as the water level rises inside their homes. Someone has posted a picture of a six-foot swamp rattler in his living room, and an hour later adds a close-up of his finger with two little holes in it. People are being unhoused no matter how hard they try to hold onto their things, and each other. I decide not to look at Facebook for some days. I want to keep from the planet's troubled corners. I also want to resist wondering if the lover I'd been here with might check to see the photographs I sometimes post; Facebook is its own portal of disembodied, virtual encounters.

During the last days of my island stay, I log back on and read that Hurricane Irma is predicted to hit the Florida Keys. It is September 9, 2017, and one post, shared from the Olympus Homeowners Insurance FB page, reads:

> "The storm is here," Gov. Rick Scott said Saturday morning, noting that the storm
> surge could reach 15 feet in some places. "Fifteen feet is devastating and will cover

your house," he said. "Do not think the storm is over when the wind slows down. The storm surge will rush in and it could kill you."

More updates:

Lisa writes:

. . . I am in Miami Shores and the first outer band just came through. Rain and wind hitting hard. The lights flickered but stayed on. How is everybody?

Elizabeth writes:

. . . Good-night, Juchitan, Mexico. Good-night, Barbudo. Good-night, Caibarién, Cuba. Good-night, Columbia River Gorge. Good-night, Bangladesh and Burma. Good-night, Overseas Highway and 7-Mile Bridge. May we wake, soon, and not have forgotten one another.

May we not forget one another, and yet we will forget one another, gradually, maybe necessarily. The August we were on the island my then-lover and I had planted a succulent on his late mother's birthday. He had said, with consternation, that he no longer remembered her voice. Now it has flowers. I hear goat bells and the figs hang ripe and too full on their trees, yet I keep looking at the pictures Lisa posts. The sky in Florida is a rolled carpet of indigos, swathes peeled back in lavender and black layers. I leave the computer and watch the cats. An anarchic vine has magically rooted itself in a pot and keeps sprouting tomatoes. When I log back on, I read: "In Port Arthur, Harvey Continues Path of Destruction."

Disasters connect us. This seems to further emphasize the "strange but true" fact—as described by the Italian writer Natalia Ginzburg regarding another precarious time, in fascist Italy—that the ability to communicate our despair in these moments keeps us "intimately linked to one another's destinies." Is this sense of connection why I keep logging onto FB despite the fact that I am on the island to forget the world, and to reconcile, too, what the house and the island still held of happier, less lonely moments? There is a Greek expression, τί μας βρήκε (what found us), used when disasters befall us, finding us unprepared. I imagine this is part of what Ginzburg means when she describes our destinies as connected by efforts to communicate: that "egotism has never solved despair." When we fail to find symbiosis—that Greek root again—our living becomes mortally sick.

Nero is outside the kitchen door. She's looking at me look at her through the screen, her large, yellow eyes unblinking. My cat seems to notice and positions herself at the door, so I open it. Nero, the more poised, stretches. When my cat lets out a low growl, Nero walks away to lay herself at the bottom of the bougainvillea where the dirt is cool.

I find this scrap from Adorno's *Minima Moralia* in my journal from when I was at the house last Easter. Our readings are their own conversations, or meta-conversations, with the lives we are living. There's no larger context for the quote in my notes, so my reason for having written it is now unclear, but it speaks to me:

> Nothing however is perhaps more catastrophic for the future than the fact that soon literally no one will be able to think of this, that every trauma, every unprocessed shock of that which recurs is a torment of coming destruction.

What was "this"—this "every unprocessed shock" and "every trauma"? It's chilling enough to read "that soon literally no one will be able to think of this." Though here, where Maria will come with eggs, and Giannis will explain how to protect the wood, and Xristodolos tells me "not to worry him," a collective ethos continues. These gestures, an homage to what still lingers in more rooted lives, remind me of how the traumas of loss might be assuaged. Maybe by "every unprocessed shock," Adorno is speaking of the failures of language to reconnect us. On Patmos, for Maria and Xristodolos, my sheets and house repairs were part of a shared continuum: moments I would have long forgotten without them and learn to understand as a ritual of upkeep meant to house us all.

The night I leave to return to Athens, there's a half moon.

I read of another hurricane watch. CNN is describing Hurricane Maria as having left "apocalyptic conditions" in Puerto Rico. The report says the island is "without power and communications . . . millions of people, including city leaders and first responders, have been cut off from the world since Maria hit Wednesday."

Puerto Rico—an island paradise turned into an island nightmare—cut off from the world, the reporter says, as an indication of the extent of the nightmare. I'd been reading Judith Ortiz Cofer's *The Cruel Country*, in which, on her way to her mother who is dying of cancer, she describes an aerial view of Puerto Rico:

> . . . at such a low altitude . . . I get to see the Island's full natural beauty from the vantage point of a seabird . . . stunning turquoise of the seashore and, ahead, mountains so lush that in spite of the weight of the word *cancer* growing in my chest cavity, the poisonous taste of it on my tongue, and the bubble of sobs on the verge of choking me, I let out a sigh. A Puerto Rican sigh.

From the plane, Cofer's vantage is a lesson in perspective. Of her mother's years in the mainland US, Cofer says, "her ability to cope with life in a country she would never accept as her own depended on these periods of diving back into her Island culture . . ." Are these returns to our geographies of love what keep loss from undoing us, what give us refuge? *"Ponas to nisi"*—"πονάς το νησί" ("You pain for the island")—Markos had said as a way of telling me I was part of the island in a way that kept it close to me.

That last evening, I walked the stone pathway where the fruit of the neighbor's fig tree covered the stones. Bees were everywhere. Nero stayed perched on a wall, her black fur blending in with the trees. I almost didn't see her. It was her gem-yellow eyes that gave her away. She had not come to the house; maybe she understood I'd be leaving.

Back in Athens, I have a Lampi stone on my desk, and a white quartz rock from the island of Thasos where there was a fire two years ago. The quartz fits perfectly into my palm, and I have the impression it has grown smoother, more transparent, from my handling of it. I'd also picked up two charred acorns and a piece of burnt pine; I wanted to be reminded of the places where I had found them. Genese Grill says, "objects make us dream," and these pieces reassure me.

I get an email from Frances in Puerto Rico:

> *I'm fine in Cabo Rojo, the west side of the island. Today with power and internet in my office, but no power or water at home. My cel [sic] is 99.9% of the time incommunicado. But we are fine, thank you for your concern and messages . . . I send you all my love. Un abrazo fuerte*

This makes me cry. None of the media's spectacle put me in Puerto Rico the way Frances's *un abrazo fuerte* had me with her. She sent *un abrazo fuerte* despite it all or because of it all. Because of it all, some were on rooftops trying to get a signal; some without electricity and running water. Closer still, between the Turkish shore and any number of Greek islands, the refugees on boats in the Aegean are trying to get out of war zones. The proximities of catastrophes become less about geography when we're relaying them to each other. "*Psyhi mou*," Maria had said, telling me of her brother, and I felt the weight in her words.

Another hurricane, Ophelia, is on its way to the Azores. I pick up my rock quartz, comforted by the weight of it in my palm. Like my Lampi rocks, it's a reminder. Unhoused, we will look for what we might latch onto. "How's everybody?" Lisa had asked on Facebook as Hurricane Irma was approaching, her overture a reminder that it is each other we look for in our devastations, if for nothing else than to reassure ourselves of life. In Etel Adnan's *Night*, she writes, "A body when dead will never warm ours, and the sea will never cry over it, and time will become its bride." And so it is in our offerings that we extend something of the soul, or *psyhi*, and hope that what remains continues to warm us. Until my then-relationship gave me a book of Adnan's, I had never heard of her; it's still one of my favorite gifts.

THE WIG & THE SCREAM, A FORENSIC

The systems I believed would end my loneliness amplified it . . .
—Anne Boyer, *Garments Against Women*

1.
There's the young migrant woman, a mother, with her baby and husband, staring at the tarmac on arrival in Zurich.

There's a Viber note mistakenly sent to me by an ex-lover that reads:
How's my baby today? Good morning love.

There's a policeman pulling me over.

There's my friend in Philadelphia with her things packed in boxes for the past 2 years, her husband in an affair he's left and returned to for the past 3 years.

2.
Hannah Arendt said *"In order to rebuild one's life one has to be strong and an optimist"* ("We Refugees").

Being back in touch with my ex didn't make me an optimist but I started to feel all was not lost.

I am on my way to my friend in Philly unsure of what I will find. My friend is probably the person I've spoken to the most since we met in the mid-1990s.

At the Athens El. Venizelos airport, the woman in jeans and a hijab bounced her baby in her arms as police checked papers and flashed a light into the baby's eyes.

3.

My friend in Philly is hoping that my visit will help heal something of her troubled marriage.

As the Greek cop pulled me over on that night road, bewildered then terrified I later thought of my friend, how she must have felt when she found the phone messages.

Love includes a measure of danger, dangers & risks that are also a part of the love of freedom.

I was relieved when I saw the migrant woman in Zurich; she had made it through, crossed the border into northern Europe with her husband & baby.

4.

When I visit my friend, we watch murder movies. *Killing Eve* is a favorite of hers. I rarely watch TV. but I saw *The Killing* on a visit during its first season.

I tell her, "He's the enemy," surprising myself at the vehemence of my words. She hopes her husband & I will talk, that it will be an opportunity for a bridge.

There were forty-four episodes of *The Killing*. She had downloaded all of them for me to see.

My ex & I were sometimes in touch. In the two years since we had split up when I was in the US, I thought of him, so I was thinking of him.

5.

An approximation = a rough measurement of, for example, hope or the unexpected, as in Julia Kristeva's idea of *jouissance* (bliss).

The policeman waved me over. I was shaking. He wanted to see my papers. I had no idea I had crossed the double lines; it was dark & the lines faded.

The number of dead bodies is part of what the cops were trying to figure out in *The Killing*, a series about murdered teenage girls in Seattle.

My friend would ask her husband where he'd been when he was away for a while. She found two phones, one behind an amplifier discovered by their dog, Bud Bud.

6.

I was in a hurry; too often I'm in a hurry. The road was dark. The policeman came out of the dark. "What's wrong?" I asked. "What's wrong?" he repeated. "You'll see."

I was in a hurry as I punched in a note on the phone to my ex.

In Philly my friend was eager that I see the whole series. "Who is it?" I wanted to know, but she wouldn't tell me; the killer is never anyone you suspect.

At some point, she told me her husband wore a wig.

7.

In the three years my friend's husband was having his affair, he left and returned eleven times. One of the times he was back in the marriage his lover sent a postcard.

"Don't you see those double lines in the middle of the road?" the Greek cop said. "No, I don't," the white double lines were as gray as the asphalt.

A truth is approximate to how much we are convinced of it. My friend's husband had no idea why there was a second phone behind an amplifier.

A halved blue Viagra tablet was on the carpet. He said, "It probably fell out of the pocket of one of my music students."

8.

The Greek cop is blunt, taking my license. He tells me in Greek, "The double lines are like *a wall*!" He is irritated & vaguely sadistic.

The migrant woman at the airport was trying to cross a visible & invisible line to what she imagined to be freedom.

Tonight, the wind is bending the trees like rubber bands, the violence of such images often suggestive of the effort of freedom, also of *jouissance*.

"Don't give it away," I'm saying to my friend between one of *The Killing* episodes, "that small ledge of yourself you've built back."

9.
Do boundaries provoke or inhibit desire? Any Freudian will say both, of course.

The instinct to protect ourselves begins with the body's bone & flesh vulnerabilities as much as its heart.

Jouissance might be a pleasurable transgression (as in orgasm), but what a transgression is (those double lines) isn't always clear.

My friend said her husband was very careful when he removed his wig at night; he put it in a bathroom closet on top of a toilet paper roll to keep its shape.

10.
When Arendt speaks of the optimism necessary to rebuild a life, she is suggesting the necessity of hope, that there are pragmatic consequences.

What happens if your hope lies on the other side of a wall? Maybe the answer is just as pragmatic—*find a way to get there.*

My friend's husband's lover was hoping the marriage would fail, which it did, but on the other side of that wall was a man who needed to hide.

The 17 young girls in *The Killing* whose dead bodies float in garbage bags in a pond were hoping for a different life (not to sound ironic).

11.

11 times my friend's husband left & returned. I watched all 44 episodes of *The Killing* on a couch. During one episode my friend's husband stood next to me.

"You see!" I looked up. "What?" He nodded to the stairs where my friend had disappeared. "Do you want to sit down?" I asked when he shook his head.

The poet Airea D. Matthews, whose collection *Simulacra* won a Yale, tweets: *Speak out for truth even if it jeopardizes you in some way.*

I was watching what was jeopardizing those in *The Killing,* so I called out my friend's name.

12.

"It was Bud Bud who led me to the phone behind the amplifier," my friend says, of her now dying much beloved dog.

She remembers me calling her from downstairs, her husband next to me saying, "See, this is what she does . . ."—meaning, to disappear.

Ironic verb, in those 10 of 11 times he left, my friend was visiting her daughter in California, she'd return to find her husband, & his things, disappeared.

"Are you moving?" A neighbor had seen a white SUV in the driveway, a blond woman & my friend's husband putting things, including amplifiers, into it.

13.

Viber & Skype bleeps made me think of my ex because he lived on another continent. There was an *eros* to the sound, a *jouissance.*

My friend did a Google map search of the lover's address & saw a white SUV in her driveway, behind it my friend's husband's Mini Cooper.

Her husband often asked, "When are you going to be home?" And she would answer, "I'm not sure."

There is a poverty to desire that insists on its object & only that.

14.
In *The Killing*, most of the teenage girls who are lured and finally killed have run away from broken homes.

My friend finally left the house she had lived in with her husband, the garden in full green. It was June.

She was crying putting in mulch with the marigolds, saying "It's for someone else now, which is fine, it just makes me sad."

The house was left with holes & cuts through its ceiling to remove "the knob & tube" electrical installation there since 1914 when the house was built.

15.
We had started to call her husband "The Wig." My friend felt some clips at his nape when they first began to date.

"The Scream" is what we called his lover because an unsigned postcard was sent to their home with Edvard Munch's *The Scream* on it.

"I tore it up," my friend says. Did the girls in *The Killing* get a chance to scream?

16.
"He can't walk the dog and talk on the phone at the same time," my friend tells me. Rather, that's what her husband tells her.

The neighbor says, "He was always on the phone."

There were, in the end, 4 phones with different passwords. He would walk Bud Bud & call The Scream.

What are we hiding from if not our most salient desires when they are the least salubrious? Everyone in *The Killing* is a suspect except for the true killer.

17.

"I called him a wuss," my friend says. "We went into old patterns. When you get to know each other well you know where it hurts."

Maybe the mistaken Viber message from my ex had to do with the fact that he knew where it hurt.

To rebuild a relationship (situation, nation, etc.) requires a cool look at what's broken for that strength & optimism Arendt speaks of.

The poet Maggie Smith tweets: *Stop expecting the worst: at least as many things could go right* . . . This assumes a basis for what *could go right*.

18.

I had hoped being back in touch with my ex would create a bridge. We used to laugh a lot & be exclusive until he wanted to be less exclusive.

"I want my marriage back," my friend says when I ask what she wants from a man who has been serially unfaithful.

Forensics takes account of all the evidence. Clues build a case, making visible what has remained in the dark.

My friend's husband removed his wig in the dark "very carefully," my friend says. "What about during sex?" I ask.

19.

It is so often dark in murder scenes, & women so often cornered in that darkness.

My friend had questions throughout the 3+ years her 15-year marriage was in crisis. Her husband would say things like, "Nothing is permanent."

I asked, "Did he say including his hair?" She says, "Plastic is eternal."

Speak out for truth even if it jeopardizes you in some way becomes more loaded when your truth crosses another's. The Scream had her truth, too.

20.
The law is there to protect something as close as possible to an objective truth, to "right a wrong."

I wondered if The Scream knew about the wig.

"It was probably part of a 'let's share our vulnerability moment,'" my friend says. "He's going to tell her, 'Well, I don't have *all* my real hair.'"

I am laughing to the point where I have tears in my eyes.

21.
Apparently, my friend's husband's mother tied plastic bags over her head when she was depressed. She says, "He probably thinks I'll be doing the same."

They had a "5-year plan" for aging. My friend's husband's brother who was also in their band stopped going on stage because of his balding head.

It was my friend's husband's ex-wife who had suggested a wig.

I tell my friend it's important "to come clean," in any relationship. A phrase my ex had used. There is *eros* in coming clean.

22.
The law requires obedience for the promise that it is there in good faith, to protect our flesh & bone vulnerabilities.

My friend's husband had repeated *Till death do us part* 4 times in the 4 marriages he has had to date.

What happens when a law becomes outdated, or a marriage can't live up to its promise or one person's desire becomes another's murder?

In *The Killing,* those representing the law are among the guilty.

23.
Sometimes a truth is beyond the law the way a reality is beyond the available information.

If evidence is hidden there's little hope for understanding more than the obvious, i.e., what looks like hair but isn't.

The Greek cop saw double lines I didn't see because it was already a fact to him, a fact I had to look for in the dark.

When my friend & her husband were trying to save their marriage, they played a card game. She says, "He picked the Divine Child as his archetype."

24.
Perhaps the migrant woman I saw staring at the tarmac at the Zurich airport was trying to see into her future.

There were other choices in the cards, "The Wounded Child" and "The Abandoned Child," but my friend's husband saw himself as "The Divine Child."

"You don't have to get personal," my ex had said when I accused him of "pontificating" in front of a group of people.

He was right. But I'd felt slighted too.

25.

As my friend emptied the house, she found photographs of her husband in his band, *Jagger*, when he & his brother still had hair. She threw them all out.

"I imagine he's telling The Scream how I was always complaining," she says, "that I wouldn't trust anything he said anymore."

I try to help her see him for what he is, but she also sees the good times they shared.

"He's a geezer with a wig," I say, "who thinks he's a rock star at 68 starting over with a 53-year-old groupie, who tells *you*, who weighs 107 pounds, to do more sit-ups."

26.

The girls in *The Killing* are runaways, one of the most heartbreaking is Kallie. She wants to stay with her mom on an evening her mother's boyfriend is over.

Her mother's boyfriend also comes on to Kallie—*who are we hiding from if not our most salient desires when they are the least salubrious?*

My friend's husband's ex-wife had breast implants that went bad; I said something about their causing her cancer & he tells me what a good relationship they still have.

How our desires can triangulate how patterns will pattern themselves.

27.

"You can't go to couples therapy and lie," I tell my friend in another effort to convince her that the marriage is over.

She tells me he's done what he's always done, started a relationship while the marriage he's in is floundering.

"Such an old, boring story," I say. "Men and their penises."

To rebuild a life, one needs some optimism (Arendt). My friend drove me to the airport; when she returned her husband had left again.

28.

Every time my friend's husband returned to the house she hoped for a better tomorrow.

Every time she began to trust him, he would do or say something like, "Don't put the couch too close to the wall: it will mark it."

I am laughing again. My friend is laughing too. "I was like, *who* is telling him not to *mark* the wall with the back of a couch!"

Intimacy will reveal the less salubrious aspects of our needs, but when bald facts are camouflaged it's hard to know whom you're dealing with.

29.

I had not seen my ex in over a year. He could make me laugh unexpectedly; as light as I could feel, I was weighed with questions.

Why, I wondered, did he come so fully into my life to leave it so suddenly?

The Killing, as with all thrillers, builds its thrill around the unexpected—another kind of *jouissance*, or its perversion?

"You'll see," the Greek cop said, and I felt a cold fear; I'd expected him to understand that I had not seen the double lines.

30.

My friend had expected her husband would want to save the marriage, but that had more to do with her projection.

The law is one of those things, like the future, that we assume will give us a chance. *Hope dies last* is a favorite Greek adage.

Kallie in *The Killing* was hoping her mother would be there for her.

Her mother keeps disappointing her—but Kallie still hopes—her mother is her mother, after all; as my friend would say, "He's my husband, after all."

31.
We were involved, and quite intensely, my ex and I, though that doesn't guarantee anything, least of all a future.

Perhaps the depth of an involvement is as much about what's at stake in a projection, i.e., the migrant woman's hope of crossing into a more democratic Europe.

Facts can unveil realities that prove themselves very different from what we expect.

My friend's husband might have been seeing other women all along.

32.
James Skinner, the police chief in *The Killing*, used to be Sarah Linden's lover. Linden, the detective, is hot on the trail of the murders.

Stephen Holder, her partner on the case, suspects the murderer might be a cop.

When the person closest to you could be the one most dangerous to your well-being, you are in the midst of a thriller.

A border, emotional or otherwise, means an increased proximity to possible danger.

33.
Being in communication with my ex felt natural, as if no time had passed. Yet time had passed.

I was careful in my messages but present. I got a love song over Viber & was tempted to send a smiley emoji.

It was meant for his teenage son who wanted suggestions to send to a new girl-friend. That was the story, anyway.

Policing myself did not come naturally. That's the point the Greek cop was making: *the double lines are like* <u>*a wall*</u>!

34.
Sarah Linden was about to move on to Sonoma, CA, & away from detective work, when she was drawn into the case.

Patterns are often mysterious even when they are obvious. I managed to see all 44 episodes in 2 sittings.

Forensic: . . . *examining the objects or substances that are involved in the crime* (Cambridge Dictionary).

Some objects: a wig, an unsigned postcard of Munch's *The Scream*, Viber messages, packed boxes, Viagra tablets, cell phones.

35.
When you're too close to a situation, it's hard to see the pattern, to make out facts like double lines on a night road.

Sometimes it takes multiple killings before a pattern emerges. Seasons 3 & 4 were added to the crime series.

My ex liked to send me songs when we were involved.

When I saw the YouTube link on Viber, I smiled, if not exactly with *jouissance*.

36.
It turns out there were a lot of wrong turns in the search for the killer. There isn't just one killer, though there is a main suspect.

Our assumptions can cost lives, as in *The Killing*, as in the rejection of those seeking refuge.

So many refugees assume the free world will welcome them, & so many have found death.

Maybe The Scream sent *The Scream* because she found herself in a place where she felt a danger.

37.
For the Ancients, catharsis, a "coming clean," required an ability to see a situation for what it is.

Oedipus gouges out his eyes because what he sees is overwhelming, & in blindness earns in-sight.

"I imagine The Wig is telling The Scream that I was 'always demanding something,'" my friend says.

"So, she'll try not to ask him for anything," I say. "Then he'll tell her how calm she makes him feel, & there'll be more postcards of screams."

38.
Besides the 17 murdered teenage girls, there's Ray Seward, also a victim wrongly convicted, & hanged.

After I'd said my ex was "pontificating," I tried to patch things up, but he was angry. He texted: "Oh, everyone noted it—'she really went after you.'"

Proximities to vulnerability increase the stakes of what can be found out.

Think of ICE turning up in the middle of the night, separating families to deport the undocumented.

39.

Law & Order is another of my friend's favorite series. She left the house with its holes & cuts & blooming marigolds in the garden.

Oedipus banishes himself in an acknowledgment that order must be restored, & he the source of ill.

It was at the airport that my ex & I were texting, "You wanted to lash out at me for whatever reason—you were angry!" he wrote.

We argued different takes, "Who cares that you like it," he said of the writer's work we disagreed on, ". . . you couldn't just argue the merits."

40.

It was the murdered Kallie's ring on Skinner's finger that allows Linden to recognize him as the killer he is, rather than the lover he was.

A break in a pattern invites a remapping. If patterns are entrenched, systematized, i.e., ICE, i.e., starting affairs in the midst of a crisis, a challenge = a violence.

I was losing the ability to distance myself.

My messages on Viber were hurried, full of misspellings. I would soon be a continent away.

41.

To seek a truth, to rebuild a life, to find the strength means to put yourself in jeopardy, i.e., you don't get to hide.

I crossed the Atlantic. In Germany waiting for the connection to Athens, I hear the Viber bleep, feel a *jouissance* (my ex?).

My friend left the boxes she'd kept packed for 3 years, & her wedding dress in one of them.

She moved to another city with her beloved dog Bud Bud, who was full of tumors.

42.
The proximity to change = vulnerability = a break in a pattern = a chance to come clean.

Sometimes timing is everything. I kept urging my friend to leave, saying it was dangerous to stay.

My misspellings suggested a danger. "When are you going to start calling me a silly . . . floppy [I meant sloppy] thinker," I wrote my ex.

He repeated, "You couldn't just argue the merits." He was sticking to his side of the double lines.

43.
Stephen Holder realizes Linden is onto Skinner. It's not clear if he's afraid she'll be killed or that she'll kill Skinner.

Everything is familiar & isn't. A year after my friend had moved away, she got an email from her husband saying it was their wedding anniversary.

Sarah Linden shoots Skinner who seems to think she'll still see him as the lover he was, rather than the killer he is.

Everything is familiar & isn't. The Viber message from my ex read: *How's my baby today? Good morning love.* A second later: *sorry.*

44.
The dark is also where dreams are seeded, where I saw an empty stretch of road & a Greek cop saw the law, where my friend saw the chance of a new beginning.

Was the *sorry* a bridge or were my ex's words meant for someone else. Some days later I texted back, "This wasn't meant for me, was it?"

In our day, in America, a land meant to represent so much freedom, children are put in cages when they cross a border.

My ex replied, "No." I'm still not sure if the Viber message was deliberate, a way to mark a boundary, a killing.

MAGNOLIAS

Each body, each moment, each site of the present
attaches to a body both individual and collective.
—Susan Briante, *Defacing the Monument*

The Lamb's Ear petals had dried. I'd put several leaves of them into my carry-on, but it was six months since May when I made the trip from Athens to my parents in Atlanta. I was using the bag to travel again. There were bits of still-soft petals, still that pale jade I loved when I picked them from my sister-in-law's garden in Atlanta. I was going to be in Providence, Rhode Island, for a week. I opened the bag at the bed-and-breakfast as shreds of the Lamb's Ear clung to my folded clothing. In May, my older brother David and I had agreed to meet up and spend a week with my bedridden mother and aged father. My mother had had a stroke and my father was ninety-three. They were in a facility next to my younger brother George's family in Atlanta. He and Emily, my sister-in-law, had the responsibility of looking in on them, but they would be going on a trip.

The Lamb's Ear petals were a reminder that I had not written the essay. I carried the petals like a talisman. In the US again, the feelings from my May visit returned, the sense my brother David, who lives in England, and I had had, that we didn't think we would see our mother again, that we had said our individual goodbyes. My father, controlling and oppressive in our childhood, was controlling and oppressive in our adulthood. We'd plotted how to find time to be on our own with our mother. My time would be when my brother took my father for a supermarket run. David's would come after lunch when my father routinely went for a nap. Routine was religion to my father, as were his naps. They kept his demons in check, or so we thought.

I'd forgotten, or lost, things on the trip to Providence, and lost things when I flew to Atlanta in May. A knit cap made by a woman on Innis Oirr, the Aran Island, forgotten in the bed-and-breakfast. I went back into the room where I was staying to look for it only to realize it was on the receptionist's table in her now-locked room. A pair of headphones given to me by someone I'd been in love with, forgotten under the plane seat in front of me. Their black case blended in with the carpet, and I'd forgotten to check before leaving the plane. I missed them not least because they were from someone who had taken the time to pick out a gift he thought would please me. My therapist once remarked he found the fact that I regularly lost things an unconscious effort to rid myself of experiences that amounted to who I was. Perhaps I yearned for a less burdened self. Maybe the losses preempted disappointment by provoking it. Another way to travel light, shed what I was too heavily attached to.

In "On Keeping a Notebook," Joan Didion reminds us that it is good, even salubrious, to revisit one's past selves. In George and Emily's beautiful home in Atlanta, having flown there from Athens, I reencountered the self that had left the US to live in Greece. My two brothers and I were born in Saigon, now Ho Chi Minh City, but when the Viet Cong readied to take over the city, my father moved us overnight to Bangkok where we lived for seven years before settling in Greenwich, Connecticut. It always felt awkward to explain this when anyone asked where I was from, or where I'd grown up. People don't generally expect complicated answers to polite *Where are you from?* inquiries. Perhaps my therapist was right. Perhaps I wanted to remove the layers of so much identity, breathe in a less encumbered present.

But in this present, my mother has had a stroke. My father turned ninety-three in March. Since my mother's first signs of dementia almost a decade ago, he has spent his time caring for her. Born in 1926 and having fought a guerilla war against World War II–era Nazism, he was still, so often, appallingly patriarchal and controlling. All my life I have most consciously tried to be someone that was not him; though I returned to Greece, the country that exiled him after its Civil War because as a guerilla fighter he had affiliations with the Communist-backed Left. He, instead, would simply say, "We just wanted to defend our country."

I had traveled for over twenty-four hours to get to Atlanta. The bed I'm finally in is plush, the sheets the best of American cotton, as the ads will say, a bliss of comfort. George and Emily are very generous. Emily is amazing in the seeming effortlessness of the way she cares for my parents. I say this because she has not been schooled in the sometimes-oppressive assumptions of familial caregiving that is particular to Southern European families where aging parents often live with the families of their sons or daughters. The first morning I'm at the house in Atlanta I go into the garden. Emily has added plants since I last visited. "That's Lamb's Ear," she says, "they must have that in Greece," and I shake my head. I cut one of the leaves to keep by the bed I'm sleeping in. I rub its furred green against my cheek, the softness a caress. When we leave for the facility, I put some leaves in my pocket. On the facility's third floor, I find my mother in a wheelchair, her head thrown back, framed in its white spread of hair. I burst into tears. Her eyes register that it is me. Me, and my brother David. The stroke has left her unable to walk or care for herself. Maybe she is lost to us, but when I squeeze her hand and say, "Mom, it's me," she seems to nod.

In the afternoon I am staring at the hydrangea flowers in Emily's garden, their deep blues and near-lilac colors. Emily had told me not to bother watering them since she was going to build a new deck, and most of the plants would be uprooted and rearranged. I'm surprised at the ease with which she's already turned the house into what it will become. I mention my mother, that I think she understood who I was when we saw her in the morning. I tell Emily she had moved slightly forward in her wheelchair, "like a plant bending toward the light." Emily says that after the stroke, my mother had been entirely absent. That it was hard to wash and dress her. Emily bought several nightgowns and was perplexed that the caregivers on the floor had picked the one with no buttons but managed to get her arms and head through the neck hole.

For the seven days George and Emily are away, my brother David and I go to the facility. It's high-end. I think of it as a luxury hotel for the aged. Like the hydrangeas in Emily's garden, these aged people were once in full bloom. The women especially, but the men too, look like plants that need watering; their thin arms and legs droop by their sides or over their chairs and wheelchairs. My mother is collapsed in her wheelchair the second morning David and I arrive. How is she experiencing her body, the mortality we see so visibly? She opens her eyes and says to my brother, "You remind me of my son," it is the one sentence we can make out. The other, I think, is "I love you," just under her breath. My father sits for hours holding her hand. He gets up and says, "Look at me now." It is unclear to me if he's addressing her, or David and me; he kisses the tip of my mother's nose, a perfectly straight line of bone. Her hands are still lovely, the nails painted a light ceramic color.

Outside the windows of the facility is a city in early summer, Atlanta's heat, and the magnolias I never tire of looking at. I think of them as gifts, the white-flowered blooms a surprise amid the trees' thick greens. At lunch my father orders the same thing for the seven days we visit: grilled shrimp with broccoli. The apartment he and my mother have been living in is two floors below the intensive care unit of the facility. Since my mother's stroke, his days are shaped by her waking and sleeping hours; his lunch hour is the only time besides his nights and afternoon naps when he is on his own. He wants to stop by the apartment to get his bottle of Spumante from the refrigerator, chuckling as he places it in the basket of his wheeler; it is against the rules to bring anything not ordered from the menu, but the waiters and waitresses indulge him.

Watering the garden that afternoon, I want to know the names of the plants. Succulents called "hens and chicks"; Norwegian pine; boxwood; flowering quince; two-toned pink and red camellias; Japanese camellias, the hardiest; peonies; violets; the violets all hues of purple and white; "wild weeds," Emily called them, "but nice weeds," I added. A friend tells me over the phone that Lamb's Ear was used as gauze to wrap the wounds of soldiers in the American Civil War. I imagine Whitman celebrating the plant *Stachys byzantine* and pause at *byzantine*, this too with its roots in the ancient world, growing on this earth for so many centuries.

The next morning, I pass runners and overhear scraps of conversation. "In just twenty-four hours I was refinanced ..." "Yeah, the doctors were cool about it ..." I pass affluent driveways with expensive cars. There's nothing small about anything in this neighborhood. And every morning, I look for the magnolias, their shapes and blooms; the brown-edged petals of the dying flowers that have taken on a sepia hue, gorgeous, open-palmed. There are the perfectly pointed cones of newer buds, erect, erotic, some with splayed petals that make me think of white folding skirts.

Today my mother stares at me wide-eyed, and I ask, "Who am I, Mom?" I repeat the question. David had suggested we get her a stress ball to squeeze, and I put it in her hand. She doesn't drop it. When I say, "Squeeze it, Mom," and show her, she looks at me some more. She says at some point, "I have to go to the bathroom," her voice barely audible. I repeat her request for the bathroom to my father. His lips purse, "There's nothing we can do about it," he says. "It's either a catheter or we follow the routine of the floor. They know when to change her." My father is talking to David about their phone numbers, how many zeros he needs to add to call Europe. I get up and my father thinks it is to ask for my mother to be changed.

He's annoyed. "Look, we live here," he says. I say I know that, that I am going to use the bathroom myself.

Later, in the garden again, I remember how the trees looked from the window in the facility. My mother in her wheelchair next to the windowpane when there was a jay near enough so we could see its blue feathers. A squirrel approaches the seat where I am now writing, and I feel an odd panic. Will it claw me? Then I say, "Hey . . ." as it runs off. The trees outside the facility window moved in a soundless wave. My mother was following their movement, at some point I hear her whisper, "Beautiful."

No visit to the US is without a list of things to buy and take back to Greece: toothpaste (bigger tubes), Gap sale items (cheaper), books. But this time I'm less interested in stores. I want to learn about the plants I'm watering. I want to say things to my mother and think I've missed my chance, living as I have on another continent. I tell my good friend in New Jersey that what adds to the grief is the fact that I don't think we will be able to talk to each other again. The dementia has taken her gradually away, but the stroke has removed her further. "Give her permission," she says, confusing me. But then is explicit, "Give her permission to leave." This shocks me. "You're helping her," she continues, filling in my silence, "to allow herself to do something she might feel she can't do otherwise." I think about this, about what my friend says later, that she's holding on for my father. This is not implausible. In over sixty years of marriage my father has dictated almost everything in my mother's life and now, maybe, her choice to live or not. In my narrative of her, it is one of the reasons that she disappeared into dementia, a world of her own where I imagine her having unimpeded conversations with herself. I am telling my friend of the vague odor in the facility despite its high-end décor, that I leave to take walks even in the overwhelming heat, how transfixed I've become by the lush fleshiness of the magnolias. She says, "Cut some branches and give them to your mom."

The next day we have an impromptu visit. Maria, a friend of the family's that I have not seen in years, is in town. She wants to see my mother. My father had told her about the stroke. My father, predictably, feels imposed upon, his routine disrupted. I have exhausted myself overthinking my father's temperament in any given situation. But the reality was, if he got over the irritation he never attempted to hide, these breaks in his routine became opportunities for expressing aspects of himself he kept otherwise buried. He was, after all, a survivor of war. Maria had been raised in Queens by a half-sister older than herself, the first woman to graduate from the Greek medical academy in Athens just before the Nazi occupation. Her half-sister had left Greece as an émigrée with her Russian-born husband, a painter. Since she was an MD, she quickly found work in a Long Island hospital. She had no children, and eventually managed to get Maria to the US, who she raised like a daughter.

Maria appreciated my father's stories. Unlike us, she cajoled him. He seemed to relax after she arrived and started to talk of his past. It had to be prompted and we, his children, too conditioned by the parameters he had trained us to adhere to, were less at ease with the conversations that anyone else might encourage. I don't remember how the subject came up, but he was talking about the war, his years as a "partisan," and mentioned "Elias, a fellow partisan" who was with him in the Resistance. Elias was a Syrian Jew from Thessaloniki. My father spoke of the Sephardic Jews as a group the Ottoman Turks had "transported from Spain to Thessaloniki."

After saying "Elias," the Greek pronunciation, he says "Elijha." According to my father, the Nazis would round up the men in the neighborhoods, "making everyone drop their pants so they could see who was circumcised."

When we leave my father gives my brother David and I the Greek sugar-coated *kourabiedes* that Maria brought with her. And a mango. The mango is overripe. I find it's changed shape in the heat when we get back to the car after shopping. I am overcome with sadness in the midst of trying on a pair of white jeans in a Gap changing room. The face that looks back at me is sad. I see my mother in my mouth. Her smell is still with me. I had asked that the floor assistants change her; there was the same scent I had been smelling when I was sure she had soiled herself, but when she's changed, I'm told, "She was dry," and realize the caregiver is annoyed. The scent was not what I thought it was but the scent of her skin, her body, the person who looks out at me through her eyes, is my mother.

"I just *love* the magnolias," I tell my pal in New Jersey when I call her in the afternoon. "There is something gorgeously secret about them." I describe the startling flowers, cushioned as they are amid layered greens. She again suggests that I bring some to my mother. One for each of her children, she says. The thought stays with me when I take my morning walk past the large driveways of spotless asphalt. I have never seen spotless asphalt. I find several magnolias in bloom and cut them, four altogether though we're three children. I wrap the stems in a water-soaked paper towel and press my nose into their blooms, surprised at how quickly the buds begin to open; in a matter of minutes the petals open further.

When we pull into the facility umpteen tiny American flags are lined up along the driveway. It is Memorial Day. As we walk through the thick-glassed doors I brace myself for the scent. I ask David if it's only me. He says, "It's inevitable," but it's also the discrepancy between the upscale look of everything and the fact of its function as a home to the departing. I feel a threshold, my ability to concentrate overwhelmed. My mother and father are in front of the communal television, he is holding her hand; he does this for hours, in silence. Today we wheel her back into her room so we can have some privacy. There are those in wheelchairs with their heads thrown back, their eyes in wandering open gazes, the expressions haunting. As if all that remains is a question, and everyone suppliant to it. A rather attractive woman smiles at me, and I smile back. She is wearing some jewelry. Emily said my mother had been wearing a lot of jewelry before her stroke. Now her hands are bare. I notice the slight indent of skin on her wedding finger. As I'm wheeling her into her room, the woman says, "I hope you get her to say a few words to you." I pause and ask, "What?" She repeats what I think she said, adding, "You know, before she dies." I nod, surprised by the chill this leaves me. I know my mother is dying. My brother and I almost hope it will happen while we are here, we say it would be "a gift" to be present; maybe she would sense us as escorts, there to usher her on. It is the phrase "before she dies" coming from a stranger that unnerves me, our presence in her eyes, so clearly a farewell. While we, still her children, are thinking of her as our mother, always that bit more powerful than ourselves even though she is now little more than a breathing gaze.

When I'm back in Emily's garden, I water the Lamb's Ear and stare at the jade-colored leaves, the gathered droplets gemmed in light. I read that it is "a handsome, fuzzy, gray-leaved groundcover that thrives in problem areas such as dry shade and poor soils." The problem area of my heart I think, poor soil indeed, then a lizard darts up the brick next to the plants I am watering. Is it the same lizard I saw yesterday? She moves toward a cluster of lilies. I give it a name. "Lizzie," I say, "it's good to see you."

Today I decide to bring a single magnolia to replace one of the flowers that had shed its petals. My father found the gesture ridiculous, he seemed to suggest as much when I walked in with four magnolias that already looked like they were losing their blooms.

I realize I have always gauged the smallness of gestures against the largeness of my father's dismissals; if I have a politics at all it is in a somewhat absurd belief in even the tiniest intervention to the scale of what passes for largeness. "Make America Great Again," chants Donald Trump as he campaigns for the presidency. Yet his call to greatness, built on the labor of the poorly paid and disenfranchised, makes it a stolen advantage. I think of some of the couples I know, how there too someone is generally doing the major labor in the partnership. There's that anecdote about Vera Nabokov licking the stamps of Vladimir's letters. Koa Beck, in an April 8, 2014 article in the *Atlantic*, writes: "Vera not only performed all the duties expected of a wife of her era—that is, being a free live-in cook, babysitter, laundress, and maid (albeit, she considered herself a 'terrible housewife')—but also acted as her husband's round-the-clock editor, assistant, and secretary." How close to abjection can devotion find itself in its service to the scale of an ambition, whether of an idea or a person?

But it's the magnolias I'm concentrated on, the fragility of their blooms, that they remind me of how temporal beauty is. I also think of my father's sweeping dismissals that have sometimes cut me off from what I was trying to express. Maybe this isn't so far off from what happens to these blooms: Cut from their source of nurture the magnolias quickly die.

Back in the US, a year and three months since I visited Atlanta with David, and ten months since I was in Providence, I am still carrying the Lamb's Ear in a baggie, and still writing this essay. So much time later, the petals are soft shreds; also in the baggie is a dark magnolia heart—what was once the bloom's center is now a dried and darkened pod with tiny red seeds buried in its crevices. I have carried these from a shelf in my Athens kitchen where they sat for over a year, and now, newly arrived in North Carolina, they are again reminders. There were my mother's bare sounds, my father's impatience the last days of our week together. There was my friend Margot, whose mother in Canada had passed some years ago, reminding me that if it was her, she would make the trip from Greece as I wavered about going at all, always at odds with the emotions my father still provoked. And Margot enigmatically saying, "It's only words now, there's nothing else anymore," as I was finally convinced to go.

During this time the world has been ravaged by COVID. My mother, still alive, is in isolation. My father can no longer visit the floor of the facility where she is being cared for. He is furious and overcome with sadness. It is the first time that I feel unalloyed empathy for my now ninety-four-year-old father whose more than sixty years have been spent with a woman he has considered his since marriage—both in the old-world chattel sense of "his" as much as in the romantic sense of *Till Death Do Us Part*. My brother George is impatient with my tone when I point out that our father has not been outside of the facility. "It's a rule," he says. "No one goes on that floor." I ask, "What about the care workers?" He replies that they are being monitored, at least that's the assumption. But there is my father in the fragility of his age, someone who survived a guerilla war, someone unused to being told what to do, now told he cannot see his wife in a place he has paid for so they might remain together *Till Death Do Us Part*. "For all that money," I finally say, "you would think the people in charge might find some kind of solution." George vaguely agrees. The first Saturday I am in North Carolina, I call my father; his voice sounds clear, if halting. He has not seen "mother," as he has called our mom for several decades. He's upset and frustrated. My mother's caregivers put her on Skype once a week to talk to my father, but he doesn't hear well, and she in her dementia cannot speak beyond her few barely intelligible words. My brother will tell me, "They say she lights up when she sees him." According to her caregiver, she's even said, "That's my George."

In Davidson, this town in North Carolina, I feel a sense of déjà vu. The visit to my parents a year and a half ago returns in the humidity of the air, and the magnolias.

The very tall, decades-old trees spread into neighboring trees, creating a canopy as their heights reach skyward to the gods. I pause to look at couched blooms inside a gloss of leaves, the yellow seed pods mysterious in the ways they reveal themselves or don't. I have been carrying the dried heart of a pod in a baggie with the shreds of Lamb's Ear for over a year and a half. "What would you write to, if you were going to die?" A line from some notes I kept; something Anne Boyer might have written? as her name is also on that scrap. I don't know why the sentence says "What" rather than "Who." A sentence next to it: "Our smallness is what we fear so we create edifices to frame and elevate ourselves." I suspect these notes were written some time ago, maybe during Trump's first election bombast.

There are days when it feels impossible to even do the simplest things, despite the finches and jays, a cardinal on the porch outside the kitchen, besides the quaint beauty of this house where I am being put up for a teaching year. I greet spiders and ladybugs, dead cicadas that like everything else look larger than anything I have seen before, their wings clearly etched, their blue, bottle-green faces vivid. I think I might wake these dead cicadas that lay on the wooden planks of my back porch. I also meet a lizard, "Lizzie," I murmur again, so many months later. This time the lizard is green and very quick. Maybe it is the heat. Maybe the proximity of these birds and squirrels and insects is what is consoling for their reminders of the last time I was in the States. I discover a cockroach in the hallway, tiny spiders. I take the cockroach out to the porch in a napkin and find it still alive the next morning. What is also familiar is the incongruity I'd felt when visiting my parents in their high-end facility. The fragility of lives against a backdrop of cheery greetings and expensive décor. Though in a facility where they are paying for the help they are lucky to have, nothing guarantees this attention to their person beyond money; what is unfamiliar here is not animate, a world of ads and virtual reminders, the sounds my computer and cell phone make, the irksome pings that startle me each time there's a message or email. I could silence it all, and often do, but I am struggling. I am trying to understand a system I need to manage to live in a world of continual incongruities.

There's a quaint soda shop on Main Street—of course Main Street, and of course The Soda Shop. A daily menu scrawled in colored magic markers on the windowpane advertises today's "Summer Squash Pie" and "Peach Cobbler" as well as

"Grilled Cheese with a bowl of chicken noodle soup." But into my first two weeks, a truck pulls up on the corner of Main with burly men who wave posters that say HOMO SEX IS SIN and YE MUST BE BORN AGAIN as they yell into megaphones. Students on campus gather on the opposite corner with their nuanced rebuttals of MY CHOICE—NOT "GOD'S"—LOVE IS LOVE and next to a pride flag, SEPARATION OF CHURCH AND STATE and MIND YOUR OWN DAMN BUSINESS. There is a back and forth on the faculty discussion board about whether the group had the right to obstruct traffic, whether a law made this a breach of public space. I think of Athens. The Athens that boiled over under the weight of financial austerity, that transformed Syntagma Square into a hub of protestors. A poster of a noose showed the then-prime minister, George Papandreou, as the hangman for having signed off on the killing measures of an EU bailout package. A far cry from the Athens of today's New Democracy government with its overzealous efforts to turn the city into a European capital by selling city center property to corporations and wealthy buyers.

Mr. Mitsotakis, the current Greek Prime Minister, believes he is cleaning up undisciplined gatherings in a culture with a history of protests, such as the iconic Polytechnic student uprising in 1973 that toppled the military junta. The PM wants to diminish whatever might make the country look incapable of getting its act together. Though I wonder if even he knows what that means. The mayor of Athens, Mr. Bakoyiannis, is spending thousands of euros paving "The Great Walk of Athens" that displays expensively potted palm trees as Greek hospitals fill up with COVID patients who need respirators. Maybe like Americans being reminded that they are a click away from "unlocking" a "$10 reward," the Greek PM hopes Greeks too will become first-world consumers. I find myself interrupting my online reading to check the latest "Hot Sale" because a Gap ad drops over my article so that instead of raging at what is ravaging the world, I am imagining myself in a new pair of Gap jeans.

Today CVS sends updates on how many dollars I will save if I buy the week's preferred products, $4 off vitamins, $1 off any protein bar, $15 off CoverGirl cosmetics. I traipse over to the CVS on Main not to miss, as I'm being warned in more notifications, the chance to buy things I don't need. The clerk on the floor rings me up, announcing that I've saved some $6 of the surprising $132 I've managed to spend on nothing in particular, but enough to rack up $132 for three protein bars and odds and ends I will send my daughter, who will wonder why I spend money on things like lip balm and eye cream which she can get in Athens. I have become a generic consumer, what Mr. Mitsotakis might wish for, in an Athens transformed, into a center for brand name stores and businesses.

I've come back to the US in the midst of a COVID pandemic in a US election year and feel the foreboding. Having failed to protect his people from the ever-encroaching virus that he calls "Chinese," the 45th President is only interested in who, or what, will keep him in power. Meanwhile in Athens, in July, a bill was voted into law by 187 of the 300 members in the Greek parliament that will only allow street protests for those who have official government clearance. "One's freedom to protest is as valuable as another's freedom to reach the hospital, his work, or his home," said the Greek PM, which assumes that any of those protestors have access to a hospital, workplace, or home. What links the 45th US President and the Greek PM is a refusal to credit the terms of their privilege. I am thinking of my mother again, and the years she submitted to my father's will. "You don't know how to speak to him," she would say, but there was only one way to speak to him. There was never any room for protest. I am also wondering if Vera, as Vladimir's wife, may or may not have felt taken advantage of.

"THANK YOU for Loving Us Back," says a Soma underwear ad in my inbox; it turns up after I buy a bra. I'm as amazed as I am disturbed by the language. Crispin Thurlow calls this "pseudo-sociality." My browser becomes inundated with ads telling me about the "Five Products" I will "NEED this Spring," urging me to "Claim your REWARD" from the CVS ExtraCare offerings. Clarks Shoes is "honored" to have me as a customer; Bloomingdale's reminds me of what is "NEW and NEC-ESSARY" as my mind floods with images of things I would not otherwise think to purchase. They interrupt my concentration; paisley-patterned skirts and yoga tights drop over headlines of protesting Belarusians. Olga Tokarczuk, the Polish 2018 Nobel laureate for literature, describes this barrage in "The Tender Narrator" as "good news": "The flood of stupidity, cruelty, hate speech and images of violence are desperately counterbalanced by all sorts of 'good news,' but it hasn't the capacity to rein in the painful impression, which I find hard to verbalize, that there is something wrong with the world."

The "good news," according to the 45th US President, is that he is the one who can "Make America Great Again," assuming his idea of greatness is anyone else's. Never mind that in this economy you can become "salary poor" as you "Buy into Benefits," which is what I am being told by someone in HR. I scroll through a list of "Options," learning phrases that are new to me, unsure of what to insure myself against: cancer, accidents, loss of limbs—all the above? How to make sure I am not salary poor but health insured? The language is seductive, pseudo-social, and will insist on the "good news." As Amazon tells me, "We are celebrating you tonight."

In "Where Loneliness Can Lead," Samantha Rose Hill writes that Hannah Arendt made the connection between loneliness and totalitarianism; totalitarianism "organizes loneliness" as it "radically cuts people off from human connection." I call my father alone in his room in the Atlanta facility. "Dad, are you okay?" I ask him, feeling fragile when he tells me he's not doing much, "just waiting to see Mother." He tells me he goes to the floor where my mother is and stands outside the doors insisting, "I am her husband," only to be told that only caregivers can enter. The caregivers go in and out of the building while my father, like other residents, has not been out, or allowed out. Apparently, the caregivers are regularly tested for COVID—though this did not prevent COVID from eventually infecting some of the residents, including my father.

Thinkers and writers are the pulse of the moment, and those moments are in conversation even if the writers themselves may not be. I think that Susan Briante echoes Arendt's ideas on loneliness when she gives explicit directives to push back on the myriad ways capitalism has isolated us. I think of how much my father pays the facility for the care that now keeps him separate from my mother. "Get outside. Put your body in unfamiliar places with unfamiliar people," Briante tells us. She urges us to know our bodies as conduits of agency, and not allow them to "dissipate in front of a screen." But a line in Elle Nash's short story "Dead to Me" illustrates how a gesture as basic as having a newborn placed on its mother's body is exploited for profit in America's late capitalism. Her speaker tells us, "The hospital charged forty dollars to place the baby on my chest." Consumer culture will take advantage of our most fundamental needs. I think of my father alone in his room with little to do besides watch the news and think of my mother, the body he wants next to him, the body now being expensively taken care of by strangers whose job it is to keep her fed and cleaned, and separated from him. Meanwhile, it is my mother's voice I hear on the answering machine when I call my father; disembodied, high-pitched, trying to convince the person on the other end that she, or they, ". . . will get back to you, as soon as we can."

The poet Valzhyna Mort's Twitter updates on the Belarusian resistance to Alexander Lukashenko and his regime keep me oddly grounded in the alienation of these pre-election COVID days. Mort's tweets echo Susan Briante's advice to "Get outside. Put your body in unfamiliar places . . ." The Belarusians are showing us that "In the spirit of the leaderless resistance where each person steps up to be a leader" (23/9 tweet), collective bodies are a force. Unlike autocrats who rely on the repression of bodies, the collective body will keep reconfiguring itself; and it is unpredictable. My father too had been part of a collective resistance when he and his neighborhood pals went into the Greek mountains to fight the Nazi. We grew up with stories of Mussolini's invasion into northern Greece, when those in the Pindus Mountain villages threw rugs and such into the treads of invading tanks. It slowed down Hitler's plans: he had to send in the Nazi army, which delayed their advance. It was winter when the armies entered Russia, a winter that began their demise.

An October 2020 tweet from Mort: "There was an actor in one of the cells. He recited poems . . . It's so strange: here we are in prison, torn away from the world, full of fear and apprehension, but also listening to poems recited theatrically through an air vent." There are women using sanitary napkins over the vents to block cockroaches, smuggled chocolate used to write notes. A February tweet: "Journalist Katerina Borisevich writes from jail: 'Now you'll want to take me camping! I can cut bread and butter with a thread, I can dry clothes with a help of a bottle. Whatever your situation is, keep calm and don't lose your sense of humor. Humor and books help me most.'" If "poetry can extend the document" as Muriel Rukeyser wrote, the bodies of those resisting oppressions like Lukashenko's extend the poetry of resistance.

It is an overcast October morning when I wake to the 45th US President's announcements (over tweets) of things being "*totally* under control," that "we are *absolutely* going to have a vaccine very, very, soon." He speaks, and writes, in superlatives. There will be a "*phenomenal* outpouring of citizens" who will "vote in *re-*

cord numbers." The signs of those supporting Trump in this North Carolina town are large, the trucks passing with Trump/Pence flags keep honking, some blaring music. Flags are out on lawns and hanging from entranceways. The vulnerability of the social body is the body as conduit, not commodity; it is a culture's soul. A word the person who had given me the headphones I lost on the flight to Atlanta had taken issue with. "You don't believe in the idea of the soul?" I'd asked. I don't remember his answer, but the soul of a country is its people, like those Belarusians fighting to keep it alive.

It's a dark irony that Trump's voters have ignored the fact that the 45th US President's "ELECTION FRAUD" declarations are sabotaging what saves democracies from dictatorships like those of the Belarusian Lukashenko. On November 8, one of Mort's tweets shows a photograph of "the detained in Minsk" who "stand by the wall topped with barbed wire, their hands raised over their heads for 19 hours. They are watched by men holding Kalashnikovs. The couple who took these photos from their apartment window were detained minutes after the photos appeared on Facebook." I retweet Mort's tweet with the line: "Here's what happens when autocrats graduate from Twitter declarations to controlling nations." When a country is threatened by the likes of a Trump, or a Lukashenko, it's up to its people to salvage what they can of it. It's what my father and his neighborhood pals did in 1941 when they left their adolescence behind to fight the Nazis, what US poll workers did as they counted and recounted ballots.

My brother George sends a picture of my parents over email. The photograph shocks me. My mother's hair is gone, her face molted by large age spots, her eyes glazed behind her glasses. I cannot tell if she is looking at my father or nowhere, though he is looking at her, and his hand clasps hers. It has been months since my father has seen her; the one time he was allowed on the floor, he kissed her on the cheek before leaving, which freaked out the doctor. After that he wasn't allowed on the floor for weeks. How does one explain to a ninety-four-year-old man whose life has never been separate from his wife in over sixty years that he is not allowed to kiss her goodbye?

My father was infected by the virus in January 2021. We don't know how he got it as he never left the facility. I think he knew it. He was "combative," the nurse told us when an oxygen mask was placed over his face for three days. His lungs filled with pneumonia. He died on January 18. My brother George tells me that over Christmas, when the facility allowed him to see my mother in a tent erected in the parking lot, my father had a necklace for her he had ordered online, a heart engraved with their names and the word *forever*. He couldn't see very well, and she didn't understand what he was doing as he kept trying to clasp the necklace around her neck. My niece was there and helped him latch the necklace. He wanted to make sure the heart with its tiny stone was facing outward.

There are children outside my window trick-or-treating despite the town's recommendation that, due to COVID, families avoid the age-old custom; they are visiting the porches and yards of a neighborhood decorated with skeletons, witches, and ghosts. So many have died and are dying. The 45th President has turned the nation into a haunting of misinformation. My friend Margot sends a photograph of the highway she and her husband Aristidis are traveling to make it back to Provence where they live. Visiting Athens, they made an about-face in a period of days. COVID was spiking, and the lockdowns had begun again. The night road through their car windshield is as visible as the headlights will allow. Margot says she is not sure where home is—is it Athens where she yearns to be, or Provence where she and Aristidis renovated a house "in an open field"?

Cypriot refugees to England carried the seeds of mandarin trees so they could plant them and remember their homeland, but do those seeds bear the same blossoms on a London balcony? Will their scent recall the aromas of a lost garden in Nicosia? My father had a love of particular Greek delicacies. He would ask me to bring him *avgotaraxho,* an expensive fish roe, any time I visited the US; even if I wasn't going to Bethesda, or Atlanta, the places he and my mother lived in their later and last years, he would ask that I mail the *avgotaraxho* to him from whatever entry point in the US I happened to arrive at. I had wrapped three rolls of *avgotaraxho* in clothing and placed them in the middle of my suitcase on one visit to New York. US Customs declaration forms ask that we declare the goods we are bringing into the country; I checked "NO" to the question of whether I was carrying livestock. It's food, but it's not live, though the Homeland Security dogs that were sniffing my luggage might think otherwise. I held my breath. The dogs moved on. One of the officers asked if I had anything to declare. I said, "No." What would I declare were I to say as much: that my father's appetite transgressed borders? That my attempt to bring him a food to satisfy his appetite was a way to help return something of a lost homeland? I think of the white lines on the night road in the photograph Margot sent and remember another road when I was pulled over by a Greek police officer for not keeping clear of the lines. I was in a hurry, the road empty, and it was night. How easy it is to forget boundaries when propelled by an urgency. Whole families have drowned in the Aegean crossings from Turkey to Greece in their desperation to find better lives.

I had asked my students in the "Refugee Literature" seminar I taught at Davidson College to suggest differences between "a journey" and "a trip"; did "traveling" and "journeying" suggest different ways of inhabiting the unfamiliar? I wasn't sure of the answer myself. The consensus was that a journey was open-ended, and travel more leisurely and suggestive of privilege. One journeys a life, but travels to a place of interest. "Journey," interestingly, is not a verb or noun generally used in travel brochures—trip, adventure, excursion are more frequent. We concluded that a journey might focus less on a return, that it is about what takes place in the act of traveling; we know Odysseus was headed home to Ithaca after the Trojan war, but *The Odyssey* is about everything prior to that arrival. In a journey, homes are left behind, futures uncertain.

I asked the class to think about what they would take with them on a forced journey. Belongings could not burden them. We went around the Zoom room, each of our faces filling a square of the screen. Someone remarked on how our belongings framed us in those Zoom squares. Images of how much would be left behind. Things mentioned included "my cell phone," "my meds," "a notebook," "warm clothing," "a small icon my *yiayia* gave me." It was our first seminar day. Lucy smiled when I asked if she was Greek, *yiayia* being Greek for grandmother. What we might carry was starkly less than what we could see in the background of our screens.

My father and mother had had the privilege of packing up several households in their lifetime; artifacts included buddhas, celadon bowls, wooden figurines, and all manner of household goods from sets of plates to rugs, carried across continents and countries as far-flung as Nepal and Saigon, Thailand and Greece. My father's tastes were eclectic, and sensual. When he smoked, his preferred cigars were Hamlet, a brand not easily available in the US but which could be bought at the Heathrow airport; he would ask anyone going through Heathrow to bring him several packets at any one time. (There is a rumor, perhaps apocryphal, that as London was being bombed, Churchill was concerned that the shop where he bought his cigars—a Cuban brand of choice, Romeo y Julieta—was still standing.)

Maybe an attachment to artifacts says something about what connects us to what we love most of ourselves, what we want to keep of the lives we've considered most important. Masha Gessen's March 28 *New Yorker* piece "The Scattering" details Russians packing up and taking what they could in the wake of Vladimir Putin's February 24, 2022 invasion of Ukraine. Gessen writes of the professionals, the engaged youth and middle-aged, Russian historians, scientists, web designers, NGO and charity workers—in short, the majority of the country's intellectual and moral heart. Putin referred to these Russians as "gnats" to be "spit out"; that this was a "necessary cleansing" that separated the "traitors" from the "true patriots." The rhetoric speaks for itself. I was interested in how, and what, these individuals and families packed up:

> Primakova packed sixty-seven children's books and a small suitcase with clothes and two pillows. Kolmanosky brought a backpack with high-end photo equipment, a suitcase with tea and ceramic teapots, and, separately, a collection of scents. Sverdlin took a folding bike and rock-climbing equipment.

They were not packing in the midst of bombings and death, but they were saying goodbye to a life and lifestyle that had made up who they were.

Before leaving to teach in the US, I spent months packing up an apartment in Athens that I had lived in for three decades; I wanted to throw away as much as I could. So did my daughter. We both felt we could do with less of the nonessential. I'd become aware of the radically divergent contexts of what "essential" might mean while sharing time with refugees. I began a ritual of taking things out to the trash for what I called the trash selectors, usually migrant men who parsed through garbage for paper and metal scraps to sell. I selected daily gifts-to-the-trash and considered these offerings to the deity of used and discarded artifacts. I put out ceramic bowls, silver bracelets, earrings, beads, unstained table mats, belts, attractive hats. A couch and rug went to Arina's family, the Kurdish girl we had met at the squat. Two large cardboard boxes of kitchen utensils went to Judi's Syrian family of five in Pangratri, who had just been informed that the Greek government was no longer going to subsidize UNHCR-supported rents for refugees who had been granted asylum. The Nea Democratia government under Kyriakos Mitsotakis was making asylum harder to come by; Greek army patrols had weaponized the Aegean and were refusing to rescue boats of refugees.

Borders are many things, but most obviously they are thresholds. Any crossing suggests as much, a border of potential as much as a potential violence. When I showed Waad al-Kateab's 2019 documentary *For Sama* in my Refugee Literature seminar, a student commented that part of the drama in the film had to do with the fact that Syrians like Waad and Hamza did not want to leave Aleppo as the city was systematically being bombed by Bashar al-Assad's regime. Waad and Hamza al-Kateab, an aspiring filmmaker and a young doctor, stay on to help the wounded and dying. Waad starts taking videos and documents the ruin of her once cosmopolitan city. Bleeding and dead bodies, many of children, fill the screen. Waad and Hamza, students at the University of Aleppo when civil war breaks out, fall in love, get married, and Waad gives birth to Sama, to whom the documentary is dedicated. Believing themselves to be ushering in a more hopeful and democratic Syria, Hamza and Waad dedicate themselves to resisting the Assad regime, until they are targeted. Well into the fighting and Waad now pregnant with a second child, Hamza and Waad, with their baby Sama, flee. We see them dodging bombs and checkpoints as they cross the border into another unknown.

The French philosopher Anne Durfourmantelle frames the unknown as an invitation, an encounter with the unfamiliar as a potential and hospitable guest: "Is it necessary to start from the certain existence of a dwelling or is it rather only from the dislocation of the shelterless, the homeless, that the authenticity of hospitality can open up?" In Dufourmantelle's conversation with Jacques Derrida, she discusses how the habitation of shared spaces deconstructs dualities of "self" and "other" or "subject" and "object," reminding us that "the subject" must "recognize that he is first of all a guest." The squat in Athens was an example of how mutable a sense of boundaries between the self and other becomes when groups who might not mingle in their homelands now mingled. Western constructions of subjecthood tend to undermine our essential interdependence as they aspire to the values of free will and independence, but at the squat I was taught how we are all guests within the larger context of our existence. I was a visitor to these shared spaces of habitation, and as much a guest when invited to drink chai or share a meal as any of the refugees in the temporary homes they had made in the corners of schoolrooms. One comes "to speak of 'the near, the exiled, the foreigner, the visitor,' [as] being at home in the other's place," notes Dufourmantelle.

The continuum of exchanges at the squat was made up of a handful of words, gestures—a hand to the heart, a smile, shake of the head—a constant of *tashakor*s, *shukran*s and thank-yous, There was a chicken pox outbreak, periods when food had to be rationed, months during which the municipality cut off the water—and still there were games of soccer and hopscotch and jump rope, the "Baseball Thursdays" Alicia initiated with donated bats and gloves, water games when there was water and Judi filled the inflated pools she'd brought. During the months water was cut off, a stench lingered from the leaking porta-potty toilets: people's sanitary well-being was an issue. We crowd-sourced for funds: it cost eighty euros every two days to clean them, and they were cleaned, although irregularly. Pans and bottles were filled from a tap in the park opposite the squat, birthdays were celebrated, we had play days and appointments to fix teeth, Jan oversaw food distributions and Stephanie sent money from donors in the US, though water stayed scarce.

Someone distributed shoes
Someone brought a birthday cake
But no water
A woman wanted hair dye
A pigeon sat on the ceiling fan
There was shit on the basement floor
There was art on the walls
Leaflets for unescorted minors
A food delivery every Friday
A shampoo drive
Head & Shoulders a favorite
There was Kastro who cleared the pipes
Kastro who smoked cigarillos and
Pulled a hose from the street
The porta-potties were leaking
The playground smelled of piss
Kastro siphoned water from the street
He tells the municipality he'll drill
Into the public waterway
Below the pavement
If they didn't fix the plumbing
So the next day, or next night
The municipality cements the pavement
The next day
There are games in the playground
Jump rope and hopscotch
Mothers from Kurdistan in a circle
Knitting
But no water
There's hair braiding and nail polish
Six boxes of fresh fish on ice
But no water
There's a boy who nabs Judi's flip-flops
A boy who wants green sneakers

A mother who pleads *do something*
Please, the plumbing is temporarily fixed
But the pipes clog again
There are dolls down the drains
Selfies of us helping out
Sheeman who misses the green olives
Of her village in Kurdistan
There were lessons in English, Farsi, and Greek
A room Abeer turned into a classroom
But no water
And when Abeer left
There were maps left behind
Fairytales, a chalkboard, puzzle pieces
There was Mohammed's birthday
And another bought cake
Mohammed's pregnant wife who made it
To Germany
A lighter borrowed from Jahal
To light Mohammed's candles
Study-abroad students carried water
In bottles, containers, and tubs
Insha Allah I say to Mohammed
Insha Allah, God willing, we say
Next year finds you with your family
And Mohammed blows out the candles

I don't speak Farsi, Urdu, or Arabic, but I was learning about fragility and resilience. I was not risking my life, but felt gratitude that I could be useful. The nearly four years of visiting the Athens squat had taught me the difference collective efforts can make, how the simplest gestures can provide joy, however fleeting. One of the shocking things about the COVID deaths under Trump's presidency was the fact of his indifference. During the first lockdown in Athens, my neighborhood pharmacist in Agia Paraskevi remarked that she had never realized how disposable human life seemed to be in the US; the dead from COVID had surpassed the numbers of lost American lives in the Vietnam War and the Second World War combined. Margot said, "This pandemic has taught us that we really are insignificant." It taught me what my experience at the squat taught me, that our connections can sustain us, bringing apples and a pomegranate to Mohammed on Nowruz, the Persian New Year, made for a bond that continues. Danyal's twelve-year-old voice surprised me in North Carolina one August day in 2020 when he called from Sulaymaniyah, Iraq, to say he wanted to practice his English.

"So, what would you take with you? If you didn't have more than some twenty minutes to decide what to choose?" I ask my Refugee Literature students our first day of class. "Something that might help to root yourselves again?" I don't say. I walk into class double-masked, inhaling my own breath—sometimes wondering if I'll rip the mask off in a moment of anxiety and overwhelmed panic. Will my shocked students look at me as a cautionary tale? I think back to Azize's quiet vigilance, taking two buses from the Eleonas refugee camp to meet me on a designated bench outside the Paidon children's hospital in Athens with her four-year-old Hennieh. She always dressed Hennieh fashionably, with elaborate bows in her hair. She once confused the time and came too early only to return, making the two-hour trip twice to Hennieh's exhausted and unhappy tirade in Farsi. Olina, the young intern, was waiting with downloaded Greek nursery rhymes to lessen Hennieh's anxiety. Thanks to donations from Mark Sargent, an American writer living in Thebes, and Stephanie Larson, an archeologist and professor at Bucknell University, Hennieh's teeth were fixed for some 400 euros.

I tell my students they shouldn't write more than a tweet's worth of words describing what they would take; they have to think quickly. "What comes to mind most urgently?" The Greek expression, "τι κουβαλάς!"—"what are you carrying!"—often said in exasperated if affectionate reprimand to suggest we can always carry less. Ross says he would take his cat with him if he had to grab what was most precious. I post the story of Kunkush for the class. "My meds, and my notebooks," someone else says. "What about your phone? You can keep notes on it," I say. She agrees; "But journals are personal," she insists.

What would I take with me? When I was moving out of the Agia Paraskevi apartment after some thirty-two years, I was overcome with inertia. There were selves in that apartment I hardly recognized, others I wanted nothing to do with. It was a chance to leave them behind. A note I discover in a sealed envelope amounts to a will, saying I wanted my then boyfriend to have lifelong visiting rights to our house on Patmos. He'd had an awful round of bad luck, someone who'd earned free tuition to Princeton and MIT, only to return to Athens after the PASOK (Panhellenic Socialist) government's election, seduced by its promise of inclusivity and an end to upper-class rule. Yet professionals like him had been wrecked by the movement's cabalistic populism. The 2010 debt crisis was only the largest and most consequential of the many crises during their era. God knows what I was thinking when I wrote that note. Maybe I was projecting something of myself—someone who realizes the country she's given her best self to has in fact exploited her.

I am at the counter at the airport in Atlanta with my ticket to Greece. It's December 2020. My sister-in-law, Emily, has dropped me off. I'd seen my father and mother briefly in the garage of the Lenbrook facility. I'd not seen them in over a year and a half. Tents were set up for visitors. The plan had been that after the semester's classes were over, I would visit for Thanksgiving, then leave for Christmas in Athens. But my brother George, and Emily too, came down with COVID. Over the phone, my father said, "You understand why we can't see each other," and I said, "Yes." But added, "It looks like the vaccine will be available soon, and then you'll be able to see mom more often." He was hopeful.

My mother had been wheeled down from her floor where she received around-the-clock care. She was inside the tent set up for visitors. My father was there too. We would kiss each other on the cheeks, though not now. We both smiled and I squeezed my father's hand from across the table where we sat. I squeezed it again, and he squeezed back. He leaned toward my mother to adjust her mask that kept slipping below her nose. He kept touching her cheek, caressing her face. I could see he missed her. He was happy we were there. I said again, "The vaccine should be available in a month"; he nodded and seemed as relieved at the idea as we all were. I was tense about traveling; face shielded, double masked, hand sanitizer in my bag, I was lugging a very heavy suitcase. Emily kept reassuring me that we had plenty of time. When we left, I squeezed my father's hand again: "I'll see you when I get back,

Dad." He said, "Yes," several times. I blew him a kiss, squeezed his arm another time, and then Emily and I left.

At the ticket counter there was a wait. I was a comfortable hour and a half ahead of my flight. It was going to be a one-stop trip via Frankfurt, but the itinerary had been rescheduled several times due to changing COVID measures. Someone at the counter was being told he couldn't get on the plane because his PCR molecular test results were older than seventy-two hours. He was upset and confused, and young. I was hoping the woman I saw at the counter would be the one to check me in. The man telling the young man he couldn't get on the plane seemed impatient. This was the man who ushered me up to the counter as the young guy abruptly left. I handed him my ticket and waited to ask if an aisle seat was available when a red light flashed: THIS FLIGHT HAS LEFT. He turned to me, "It's arriving in Chicago right now." I showed him the schedule I'd printed out. It had been an earlier version. "Can you call your travel agent?" he said, concerned, as I shook my head, tears starting to stream down my face behind now-fogged glasses and a face shield. The flight attendant punched in numbers.

"I'm going to Greece," I said. "The travel agent is in Greece." I was suddenly thinking of the molecular PCR, whose results had to be no later than seventy-two hours before a flight, that if I had to get another flight, I'd have to find a way to get another test. That there was going to be a further lockdown in Greece which would mean being quarantined for two weeks, and I was only going for three weeks. I was shaking as the man asked again if there was any way to call my travel agent. Again, I shook my head, visibly weeping.

"This keeps happening," he said. "People are confused." I murmured something about needing a Valium or a drink. He smiled. He said he was going to try to get me on a different flight. I said I'd pay for whatever it was. He laughed and said, "I'm not trying to sell you a ticket." I smiled weakly. He kept punching in numbers and looking at the screen, and finally looked up. "I got you on the flight to Washington. There are some seats for emergencies. It's only something we can do from here. The connection to Frankfurt is an hour after you land, you'll have to move quickly to the gate." I thanked him profusely, lugging my bag onto the scale to check it in. It was packed with Christmas gifts, Gap sweatshirts, a pair of Clarks shoes, Timberland boots for my daughter, vitamins, bottles of Louisiana Hot Sauce a friend requested, and books.

"You're overweight," he said. I nodded. I knew I was overweight. "I'll pay whatever it is." Already exhausted by the trip that had not yet begun, I just wanted to get home, though what or where home was felt unclear. I would go to my daughter's tiny thirty-square-foot apartment in Kypseli, and she would move to a friend of hers nearby. I would see my cat, Mati, who I'd missed, but home in Agia Paraskevi, the apartment I'd lived in for thirty-two years, was no longer mine.

"I don't want to charge you $200," the flight attendant said. "Can't you take out some things and put them in your knapsack?" I remember looking at his name tag, thinking what kindness, and how considerate this stranger was, how I'd misread him. I think he was from Colombia, or another Spanish-speaking country. I might even have asked him, but I don't recall. I was panic-stricken. I said I didn't have room for a toothbrush, my bags packed to the gills. He looked at me with some sympathy. "Try to take something out," he said again, and I realized I needed to make a gesture. He was doing this for me. He would overlook the $200 fee if I could demonstrate some effort to acknowledge the policy. This was more than a performance of goodwill: it was about not taking a stranger's good intention for granted. I was drained. I took half a Valium. He smiled. I think I removed two books and a shirt. I don't know what I did with them. I told him he was a guardian angel and I couldn't thank him enough. He got me on a plane after I'd missed the flight I was booked on and checked in my overweight bag without charging me $200. "Have a wonderful Christmas," I said, "and thank you so much. I can't say it enough times." He smiled again.

What was so important that I needed to carry it all with me? The trip was "a trip home" I wished to celebrate by bringing things hard to come by in Greece. The metaphysics of this came to me gradually. Things hard to come by included a level of joy and surprise in a time when joy especially was scarce. My father had known this pleasure when he yearned for the taste of the *avgotaraxho* fish roe and Hamlet cigars. The daughter of one of my father's US embassy acquaintances from his Saigon days shared a memory of my father sending a package of mangoes to assuage the family's homesickness in their sudden move to France: "newly arrived from saigon in 1960 paris," she writes, "sisters bereft of everything we knew, when nick came home from embassy one eve with small wooden crate sent from george . . . dad pried it open on kitchen table while we circled round . . . jubilation. nestling in bed of packing straw were some prized mangoes from vietnam, our madeleines. scent of home . . . your dad knew desire of the displaced person." My father knew the yearning for the tastes and scents of lost places.

Elina was waiting for me, masked, as I was. After some twenty hours of travel, having changed three planes to reach Athens, the first thing I wanted to do out of the airport was take off my mask. But I didn't. She met me with my car. When I got into my car, I was surprised by how much dust was everywhere. "The car is exactly as you left it," Elina said happily. "The car hasn't been cleaned?" I couldn't help asking. We were both confused. The car was filled with a rolled beach mat in the back seat, rubber sandals, a recycled bag full of beach stones from the past summer. Elina was a little hurt, and I was impatient. None of this had anything to do with a present made possible by a cross-Atlantic flight, a semester of pandemic-teaching, and a stubbornness to be back despite the myriad complications of getting back.

We drove to my daughter's Kypseli neighborhood. She had left the apartment key at the corner bakery and had also bought me a loaf of bread the cashier gave me with the key. Elina had cooked chickpea soup. All I wanted was to open a bottle of Greek wine and sit on the small balcony as I was reunited with the city. After finding a parking space on the cramped street and getting my bags to the apartment, I went back down for the bottle of wine. A Pakistani in the bodega, ΦΙΛΙΚΑ store, wearing a mask under his chin, rang up the bottle of *Cellar* as I eyed the single Nescafé packets and brands of chewing gum along the counter.

It was strange, and strangely magical, to return to the city I'd left so fervently. I was not fleeing in any fear for my life, but I'd left an exploitative job, an apartment with decades of life I'd put behind me, and a city overwhelmed by crises. Elina kept asking me to try her chickpea soup—a soup she knew I liked. The travel had been stressful, and it was travel—I knew my destination, knew I would be returning to the US; as the pandemic raged, I yearned, like everyone, for a space marked off from the chaos. Elina believed chickpea soup and meeting me with my car coated in the dust of the previous summer would be a comfort. My daughter felt the same, leaving a loaf of bread with the key to her apartment. My comfort was in the proximities of what I'd missed of the Athens I'd left: the crank of an old elevator, the pungent scent of cooking in the building's entranceway. Elina assumed I would want to look back, in nostalgia, to last summer. *Nostalgia*, whose Greek roots of "nostos" (νόστος), home, and "algia" (αλγεα), pain, suggested a longing turned sick with desire, something I was definitely not feeling. What is gone is gone. What we carry, or what I carried, were remnants of experience that in the months since the summer had become something else. I had no desire to return to what had passed. My tomorrow was already where I'd arrived, as Dionne Brand says, and I wanted to understand how the weeks and months since had brought me to this arrival.

What did I carry, finally, since leaving Athens in late July, in the middle of a COVID surge, months before a contested US election? I brought Greek olives and cloth masks that Layla had made; Layla the Afghan refugee mother who would also, finally, be on her way to Germany, and who I would not see again. But the colorful masks she had made of tablecloths and other fabric scraps were still with me. The image of her with a cup of tea next to the sewing machine Margot had donated is still with me. In a Zoom talk, the Albanian writer Gazmend Kapllani told our Refugee Literature seminar class that he had carried notebooks and journals throughout his life's many upheavals. He had been a refugee from Albania under Hoxha's regime and in the 1990s made it to Greece, where he taught himself the language and wrote a daily column in *Ta Nea*, a mainstream Greek newspaper. Kapllani spoke of being intrigued by households where things like family furniture were passed down for generations, by people who carried heirlooms and such between their various homes—as my parents did. For him, precious artifacts amounted to what he'd salvaged in writing.

The next morning I wander the neighborhood, mindful of the cracked pavements, dog shit, fallen, mashed olives near olive trees on roadsides. Mostly older men cluster on a street corner, several carrying plastic bags of mandarins and oranges. There must be a *laiki*, an open market day, nearby. A waft of garlic and some other spice is in the air. How far I've come from the good Samaritan at the airport in Atlanta who told me he didn't "have the heart" to charge me $200 for my overweight bag. What I'm noticing, and so grateful for, are things I might not have appreciated before I left Greece. Walking these often shit-smeared side streets, often dangerous with abrupt crevices and holes, I'm astonished. Someone with his cell phone jammed into the side of his helmet is carrying on a conversation as he rides his bike. I see chunks of bread left at the base of a tree for the strays. I see more than one instance of bread on pavements. There's dry cat food scattered on wall ledges. Clothing left out for a needy passerby. A stack of plates. Reminders of how far I am from Davidson, North Carolina, where people mindful of their leashed animals pick up their dog shit, where the pavements are smooth and clean. One young father with his toddler returned to the front lawn of my house when he ran out of baggies. As I watched him from the porch, he gestured that this was the second time his dog decided to poop. People looked settled within the parameters of lives which, like the lawns along Concord Road in Davidson, are clearly marked. There is little spill, and when there is, there are quick apologies—and someone with a baggie to pick up the shit.

As I rode my bike during those months at Davidson, several housing settlements went up. There were sweetly decorated porches, American flags of different sizes on properties. A sign on a lawn gave daily instructions: "We Are All Wackadoo-dles" or "Be Happy. It's Easier." Several "Black Lives Matter" placards stayed up. To be settled, to feel settled, an illusory privilege for any person displaced, is also what a displaced person yearns for; the signs along Concord Road spelled out the vectors of belonging, as in "Here is a space where Black Lives Matter" and "Here is a place where we are Wackadoodles"—if you enter here, you too need to under-stand these markers. When Eirini and I took photographs at the squat, we were trying to capture what spilled over the boundaries of people's displaced, or refugee, status: the children's glee during the water fights, the brightly colored collages of Mercedes Benz cars, motorcycles, McDonald's hamburgers, and bejeweled women with handsome men. These were some of the images that transgressed the fact of deprivations. They were aspirational images of joy as real as the squalor and dirt-lined nails and running noses and stench in the playground during the water short-age. Those who had found their way to northern Europe, and most of the families we knew had, shared happy selfies on social media of their smiling faces in front of shop windows and picturesque rivers and parks. "We photograph their reality at the squat," Eirini noted, "and they post pictures of their dream worlds." Maybe what I found disconcerting about the signs and flags on the lawns and porches of the Davidson homes was their explicitness: the markers left little room for nu-ance—but that was probably the point.

Margot and Aristidis traveled through Italy after taking the ferry from Patras and then drove through the night to reach their home in France. Where now is home when the contagion is traveling too, and we are its carriers—the body refuge to a virus that in some will kill it and in others is overcome? What better metaphor for our times that unbeknownst to us we find ourselves the carriers of our contagions, our bodies' passports stamped with our crossings as much as our national identities. Today the millions who have fled Ukraine carry the memory of their once routine lives in what they've managed to squeeze onto trains and cars, the images of families and children on foot, and that iconic photograph of the toddler covered in a hood and thermal suit weeping as he tries to keep walking, to say nothing of the children in Gaza, speaks to the weight of grief. "We leave to return," I say to a friend about how I feel every time I leave Greece.

Vaggeli, my daughter's father, called me the evening of January 6; he was watching the news. I learned of what had happened at the US Capitol from him. January 6 is Epiphany in the Greek Orthodox calendar, and I was still in Greece. An adolescent boy or adult man dives into the frigid January sea to retrieve a thrown cross and bring it back to the priest, a symbolic baptism the Orthodox Church preforms in "The Great Blessing of the Waters," on the day known as *ton Foton* (των Φώτων), the festival of light. Those named Theofani (God's light), or Fani, celebrate their name days. Was January 6, 2021, a deliberate choice for the failed insurrection on the American Capitol in Washington, DC, some in the mob speaking of "The Rapture," of Donald Trump's promised revelation?

Vaggeli couldn't believe what he was seeing: the storming of the Capitol by a fanatical mob was not what he knew the US to be. This was not Myanmar or Afghanistan; it was Washington, DC, and a noose was hanging just outside the Capitol in broad daylight. Epiphany celebrates Christ as the Messiah at his baptism by John the Baptist in the River Jordan. Epiphanies reveal something not otherwise visible. We had seen what Trump was capable of in his tenure as US President, but not the lengths to which he would go. One might say the same of any autocrat. To many of Trump's followers, he was the messiah of an exceptional America, with his pat slogans and pseudo-sociality.

Maybe this is what we were trying to describe in the Refugee Literature seminar that first day of class: travel can put us in unexpected danger when we lose our point of reference; the journey into uncharted space is a new border. If we're lucky—as in the chill of those freezing waters of a January morning—there might be an epiphany, some heirloom of a faith to be retrieved.

III

UN-SETTLING

One of my oldest friends visits Athens to help me pack. She arrives from New York on December 31 so we can usher in the new year together. The new year is 2020. No one knows what 2020 will bring. In the year's first hours, we smash a pomegranate in the entranceway of the apartment, a Greek tradition—the pomegranate, ancient symbol of death and rebirth, Hades and Persephone, an underworld journey that bears fruit, the fruit of blood-red seeds. Pomegranate juice splattered over the floor and the base of the wall, a red meant to bring luck, fertility, and new beginnings.

That first morning of 2020, smoke and my friend's coughing wake me. We have a fireplace in the apartment and had separated the embers before going to sleep. I follow an acrid scent into the living room and see a smoldering carpet. Burning embers lodged in the wool had escaped from what I thought was a dying fire barricaded by a metal grid. I put out what in minutes would have burst into flames. I was selling the apartment and thought wryly of what might have been on the first day of a new year.

My dreams, lucid as anything lived in my waking, journey me. There's a recurring dream of a second home on the island of Patmos. One I never knew I owned, one I rediscover with anxiety and wonder. It had a mud floor that needed to be covered. Another time there's a view from a cliffside. Once, too, I had to bend to get through a narrow, whitewashed hallway. When I was seeing a therapist, he asked what this might mean to me. It had something to do with an interior, I told him, one I didn't realize was mine, mine to inhabit and explore.

As I was leaving Davidson, North Carolina, I wrote a dream I'd had to Margot: "Strange theater scenes. A lovely inner apartment of sorts with a less upscale feel that I was renting for a short time, but was told I could, or should, buy, and most likely couldn't afford. Then a fancy group bought it and it was renovated with an intense balcony jutting over a space that was weirdly covered, but extremely impressive. A famous director was palling around with another equally famous actor or director . . . I was of course thinking of my K . . . and how chummy the insiders were with each other. A queer guy with a kind face was speaking his lines in an intoxicated, inspired state. I was a spectator, and someone was encouraging me to talk to him. I don't remember if I did but remember being impressed with the renovations and the energy and ease of these theater people. De Niro might have been there too."

Margot answers: "It is an end-of-term dream, your performance is over in this 'lovely inner apartment' of the literary world, where you were impermanently (renting) that someone told you, you should buy (make permanent) but which you don't feel you can afford (timewise? emotionally? economically? all three?) which is then taken over by a group or an individual who does this impressive superficial upscale renovation which is impressive to look at but who has not understood or noticed the INSIDE because it is still covered, i.e., the meaning, truth. You are a spectator because you are essentially not like them and do not feel that you are famous. It is all a set, paint, props, illusion. The play is finished, the run on Broadway done, you are experiencing the post-theater let down of all actors, the true and the posers, it's the end of the show."

The past couple of years have amplified endings. And the body which catalogs them becomes a sensory compass that doesn't always know how to move beyond rupture. Even in collapse the body feels for a foothold.

I tended an olive tree. I watched it grow as shoots sprouted from its slim trunk, I watered and forgot to water it. I repotted it twice. It sat outside my bedroom on a balcony. It had been gifted by a love that was no longer. One summer I was away for a while. The tree was full of tiny green fruit. When I returned, they had all shriveled. Left without water in the sun, the leaves dried up and fell, and the olives shrunk to dark specs that gathered at the base of the pot. "It's not dead yet," a friend said, snapping one of the twigs, there was green in a stem that didn't break.

In my dreams I can't always distinguish between exteriors and interiors, though there's movement, changes of scene. *I'm with family, waiting for a taxi that never arrives, it's dark. A man flirts with me. The place is smoke-filled, we don't exchange names, though I ask for his. Maybe we kiss. The scent of smoke bothers me, it's in his clothes. I leave holding something in a towel, gem-like objects spill from it. I try to find out where I am going and want to avoid people. I go up some steps, maybe it's Italy.*

After the squat on Octaviou Merlie Street was evicted on September 23, 2019, Mohammad, Eirini, and I drove to the Corinth camp the next weekend. Imported tents made of white acrylic spread across a freshly pebbled expanse. Like the tents, the pebbles were white and imported. It's a warm day and those we meet from the squat complain about how hot it gets under the acrylic. Inside the tents plywood boards separate living spaces. When the police entered the 5th School's building that Monday morning in September, they wore gloves and masks. Inside was a room of shelved coloring books, assorted boxes of glue, scissors, magazines for collaging. We had wanted to pick up the donated materials used with so much love during our visits to the squat. But the entranceway was bricked up. Sunlight entered through the glazed windows above the wall of cement bricks where someone had etched the word for shame in Greek: ΝΤΡΟΠΗ.

Where women had cleaned pots and hung laundry, sat in a circle of chairs, and talked and knitted and the children had played and chased crows, there were only crows now and pigeons and a broom against the painting of a house.

RE-

also conveying the notion of "undoing" or "backward," etc. (see sense evolution below),
c. 1200, from Old French re- and directly from Latin re- an inseparable prefix meaning
"again; back; anew, against."

—https://www.etymonline.com/word/refuge

Words are what remain, and sometimes they too are part of the debris. A single syllable like Mohammed's "hi" survives a sentence otherwise absent. He would text me when something came up at the squat and he wanted help. There was nothing else in the message until I would answer. I took that reticence as a show of respect for what I might be up to. And what I might be up to was never less important than a crisis that may have been so much more dire than anything in my present. "That *was* my home," Kevser, a colleague, says, showing me images of her burnt home in a town outside Istanbul. We enter the past tense to see the home that is no longer. Kevser sees soaked books after rain entered through the burnt roof of her ruined home. A neighbor was cooking over an open fire on his balcony and fell asleep waiting for his wife to return. The fire burned down his home and almost all of hers. Olena in Ukraine says: "I forget the names of poets I used to admire . . . it's hard for me to even remember the name of the city where I live now and what I have to do here. But the name of the man who agrees to take us on his bus to a Ukrainian safe place, and who gave my son his first piece of bread in ten days, I remember. His name was Valera."

Was holds the present hostage to what is no longer. As William Faulkner famously quipped, "The past is not dead. It's not even past." The past morphs and positions itself in what is happening now. Olena's is parsed down to the goodwill of a man who gave her son a piece of bread. When Mohammed came over to the Agia Paraskevi apartment to help me move, he remembered things because something he was doing brought it back. He picked up a large bowl and said, "We had these in my house," telling me large bowls were used to feed a family that included six siblings, his aunts, and mother who made *risokabul*, an Afghan rice dish. He describes the dish and tells me of the *lassi* yogurt milk they drank with it: it had a "lemony taste," he says. The story shapes our conversation as he smokes a cigarette and states flatly that the house was bombed, that all that stands now are two metal columns.

If we didn't tell stories, maybe we would no longer be participants in time. I write as a way to recognize myself in my present. I had, once upon a time, to build myself back from a relationship that had once built me up. Those in Gaza today are left with what was a home, and is now rubble. How will they build themselves back?

A country or nation builds itself to be included in the world of nation-states. And then there's war. And nations and their bodies are assaulted and maimed and disappeared. Borders are re-mapped, bodies sometimes manage to pass through them, many die in their life-seeking or present-seeking journeys. Many, too, attempt to stay in the locations of their belonging come what may.

A young Ukrainian woman arrived with her mother and sister in Greece with sixteen cats. I don't know how anyone carries sixteen cats, but they are with her. Just the logistics of this is a study in reconfigurations: a singular body navigates kilometers and swathes of land with live animals; the cats, like her own body, are a living present, like Kevser's love of her soaked books, and Mohammed's re-collection of his family eating *risokabul* and drinking *lassi*.

Mohammed had to make his way to Germany where Rakia, his wife, was living with their two very young daughters, the youngest of whom he had not yet met as Rakia had left seven months pregnant. He moved out of the 5th School squat as a precaution when the evictions began and managed to dodge the early morning round-up when police arrived because he was sleeping in the park opposite the school building. I'd asked him to let me know when, and if, the eviction happened. Not that there was anything I could have done, but I wanted to know.

Meanwhile in the present of that 2019 September, our group of volunteers was busy donating school supplies to the kids attending the Greek public school in the neighborhood. Some of the children, like Iman Noor, were doing very well in

Greek—she happily showed me a coffee cup with a decal of her receiving an award from her Greek teacher. I'm reminded of Ilya Kaminsky's (@ilya_poet) June 20 tweet: "Meanwhile, a friend from Odesa, Ukraine, writes that air-raid started, so ballet was delayed by ten minutes, then ballet continued. Yes, ballet performances go on. Happy Monday to you, too."

The present keeps us focused on the work of living. What happens when a present is colonized by a past being re-formed and de-formed by one man's re-collection of Peter the Great's conquests. The *re* in these instances re-fuses the present.

Mohammed texted me on the morning of September 23 a little before 7:00 a.m.; "Hi," he writes, which always made me feel like we were in a continuum of conversation. "Hi," I answer, "Everything okay?" He answers, "They come"—meaning the police. The eviction of the squat was happening, the police were orderly. The Octavio Merlie School building had housed many on their way to further journeys. Many had made it to northern Europe. Mohammed, too, though his journey was complicated. He had tried through the family reunification law, but Rakia had missed an appointment with German government officials to file. Busy with the care of a newborn, and alone, the envelope remained unopened. When she did open it, it was too late. Mohammed now needed a print copy of their marriage certificate, and his brother would have to travel to a distant village to get it, one controlled by the Taliban and dangerous to reach. Mohammed left Greece on a black passport. He called me from a camp in Romania where he'd been detained, his cellphone confiscated. Waiting was the hardest part; it made the present precarious—he might be deported to a place and past he no longer had anything to do with. He told me he passed his time playing ping pong and exercising. Over a month later he managed to get himself to the Czech Republic where he was again detained, but Kabul had fallen to the Taliban; it was August 2021 and the news was full of the botched and messy American withdrawal from Afghanistan. The present was on Mohammed's side: he had family to join in Germany, and Afghanistan was under Taliban rule.

An etymology dictionary gives this partial definition for "refuge (n.)": "from Latin *refugium* 'a taking refuge; a place of refuge, place to flee back to,' from *re-* 'back' (see **re-**) + *fugere* 'to flee.'" In the writing of events—often as they happen—I realized the journey of this book (which I did not realize would be a book) was about what creates expectation and compels the journey, not about a return to what is lost; we see for as far as we can imagine, to the next moment, or the next word, to keep present.

How does one "push the ongoing text line further"? Julia Stakhivska, who escaped Bucha in Ukraine, says, "When I left, I despaired over leaving behind my great-grandfather's written memoirs of our family—a family chronicle—which could have served as a kind of umbilical cord, a connection to something bigger than me, during this turbulent period. But then I realized: that was just a paper illusion. I still have all of these memories; my task is to push the ongoing text line further." The task is always to find ways to push whatever keeps us going.

ERASURE TIMELINE

[Cuts in Natal'ya Vorozhbit's March 30, 2022 *Guardian* article enact a visual of rupture and loss.]

"I grabbed two rings,   my mother, daughter   the cat":
fled Kyiv

Natal'ya Vorozhbit
Wed 30 Mar 2022 06.00 BST

"   reminding people that it is Russian hands pressing the buttons to release the
  Bombs   on us" . . . the theatre in Mariupol, Ukraine   a shelter
      bombed on 18 March, killing 300 people

How does it feel to be bombed out of your home   ? The author of Bad Roads
writes about   departure from Kyiv after Russia's invasion

    I took money and ID. I grabbed two rings (people   always take
jewellery). But   the cross on the wall, a family heirloom, and the painting of a
guelder rose   I chose   to guard my home and my city, Kyiv
my photos,   the portraits of two Ukrainian writers, Shevchenko and Gogol
watered all my plants,   how long will they last   Who will defrost my freezer?
my heart. Grandmother's photograph, still on the shelf. A moisturiser, a new one
in the bathroom   never even used   you stupid woman   watch   the
road.

I focus on the road   I left everything behind. I took only   my mother, my daughter and Dyusha, our pedigree cat   squealed and stank out the car all the way. It'll be 30 hours at the wheel . I'm fleeing Kyiv bombed by Russians.

    I want to sleep but the cat   shat in the car and the stench keeps me awake. What did I hope to take   ? My husband and the father of my daughter (two different men). My daughter's father is a writer—seeing him holding a gun was just weird. I left

    The chestnuts soon   in bloom without me   .

What should one pack to start a new life   I've already built?

Have you ever wondered what you'd take   if you   might never come home   ? I've been thinking about it   eight years, and more   but I could never settle   . Death is more defined   war is the end of all that's good and the start of all that's bad,   . How could anyone prepare   ? What should we pack   to take the life I've already built   ? No, we didn't deserve any of this.   , no one deserves to be bombed, to flee or to die   because the dictator   gone mad desires your destruction.

For someone   this was the last year they could have got pregnant. Someone else was just finishing   their new apartment   , welcome!). Someone had just finished paying off a debt   in the red again, another person   dying   will now die on the road, or be bombed). A child was   but   my child, you'll never graduate.

          the Playwrights' theatre,   : a theatre   for all the important words to resound. Ukraine . We put our hearts into it. Our money, too.   gone, it's been crossed out. Watch the road. Don't cry.

    Mariupol had a theatre.   . You can see the pictures, before and after bombs. Only you can't tell from the photos that under the rubble was a   shelter, with hundreds   hiding in it.   they've pulled out 300 bodies. I'll never tire of reminding people   . That it is Russian hands pressing the buttons   the bombs that fall on us. What is the point of   culture   of

nation? What is this culture we think of as great? Does this Russian culture delight
you   ?

Look at the road. Look at the road   upset, I remind
myself.   looking at the road and nothing else   we have been
engaged with   war.   we've been trying to shout to the world,   alert
them to   Russian   threat. And   after 24 February   they finally
hear us   .

We're sick and tired   , we dream of writing, making films,
talking of things   . But after 24 February, these   were closed to us,
and will remain so for the rest of our   lives   condemned to
pain, despair, injustice, death. But also   the mightiness of the human spirit,
patriotism and love.   ready.   we want to   return home, and water our
plants.   we need   help

Translated by Sasha Dugdale

TELL ME HOW IT ENDS

You become words and words become you. You do not know the difference
between utter and utterance. You will call the sea an overturned sky.
—Mahmoud Darwish, translated by Sinan Antoon

I see a thread in the books you assign
I nod, generally they're stories that have to do with movement.
—Conversation with Fatmah

"I feel the smooth, chilled sand beneath my bare feet," writes a student in my Introduction to Creative Writing class. I am reading student work this morning—October 23, 2023, another night of "the worst night of bombing so far." I need to do a job, but I keep checking Instagram posts, my Twitter/X feed; I keep trying to convince myself that it is important to do my job as the world witnesses one of the most savage assaults perpetrated on civilians. I am seeing and hearing and starting to understand the world as a deeply unjust place, and my country, or one of my countries—the country that prides itself on being just, self-described in the rhetoric invoked by Democracy's capital "D"—has endorsed the relentless bombing of one of the earth's most densely populated places. We hear, see, witness, but are unable to touch, smell, hold, or aid those suffering and dying in Gaza. To see and be exposed suggests you are unable to unsee what is seen. My student is following the feedback. My repeated advice to my class: use the sensory to evoke as much as you can of the moment, make it immersive, *as if we are there ourselves.*

A father is wailing, he cannot let go of his daughter's dead and sheeted body. A father holds the date biscuits he went to find for his young son, who he finds dead when he returns, and in his grief offers them anyway to his corpse. The smooth, chilled sand is there too as I comment on the student's piece. I listen to something blood-curdling. The night sky lights up in orange smoke. A woman, or women are screaming in utter primal terror. The Al-Shati refugee camp in south Gaza has been bombed. This is on my phone, and I am now there. I quickly turn back to my laptop, but I can't get the sound out of my head. I feel a coldness in my stomach and vaguely shake. I wonder what someone like Biden would feel if he heard it and toy with the idea of passing it on to his Twitter/X feed. I've already tagged him and others, but as a friend notes, "I doubt he reads anything on his feed." In the past sixteen days I've been on social media more than I have been my entire social media life.

In my classes, I struggle to bring context to the material I am teaching, material not always as resonant to my students as it is to me. They are for the most part non-western, South Asian, and Arab, of a world far from my upbringing and culture, as I am in the Middle East teaching in the United Arab Emirates. I am again speaking of perspective and context, two nouns that keep coming up more frequently than usual because the books I am teaching are part of a General Education program. To see outside of our ingrained perspectives is sometimes counterintuitive, I say when some of the students tell me they are not enjoying Valeria Luiselli's *Tell Me How It Ends*. The lens is on me, and it is my answers they are spotlighting.

So how does one enter a text, a room, a space of convergences where boundaries, both mutable and not, will reconfigure the terms of how to express values not similarly shared? One of the first things a student tells me is that I have mispronounced her name. When I say "FatEEmah," as she raises her hand she says "FatmAH" politely enough. I nod and repeat her name, conscious of how she has pronounced it, but I've lost my train of thought.

"Let's look at the language of the intake questionnaire," I say of Luiselli's book. I think this is a text that will resonate, as a good number of the students are from countries that have experienced forced exoduses. The classroom, where I have often felt most able to navigate the unexpected, has become a space of uncertainty; I'm not clear about how the material will be received. Many in the classroom have parents who fled countries such as Syria, Iraq, Yemen, Afghanistan, Palestine, and any number of countries from the African continent, particularly Somalia, Niger, and Sudan. A study-abroad student from the US, Peter, is also in the class, and I learn in the course of our discussions that he voted for Trump. "Twice," he says. He is one of my brightest students.

"Why did you come to the United States?" is a first question on the intake questionnaire for the undocumented that have crossed the Mexico–US border. It is followed by questions with less probable answers such as, "When did you enter the

United States?" and "With whom did you travel to this country?" The children who are being asked these questions are sometimes as young as five and six and have no idea what to say. Often traumatized by their journeys, they are generally unaware of how to articulate them. Luiselli has volunteered to help translate. "Why are we reading about the suffering of children?" Zeina asks.

My mouth was uncharacteristically quiet. I was trying to think of how best to answer. Perhaps like Luiselli, and perhaps unlike my students, I considered the injustices being described to be avoidable, and the system of a liberal democracy, like that of the United States, one that holds itself accountable. Peter raised his hand, saying he had an issue with Luiselli's tone, and cited a passage:

> As soon as a child is in the custody of Border Patrol officials, he or she is placed in a detention center commonly known as the hielera, or "the icebox." The icebox derives its name from the fact that the children in it are under ICE (Immigration and Customs Enforcement) custody. The name also points out the fact that the detention centers along the border are a kind of enormous refrigerator for people, constantly blasted with gelid air as if to ensure that the foreign meat doesn't go bad too quickly—naturally, it must be harboring all sorts of deadly germs. (22)

I asked Peter if he could say more. Like Zeina from Iraq, Peter considered what I thought a cleverly structured, heartfelt book to be "full of complaints" and "biased." He pointed out that what looks like tinfoil covering the children are thermal wrappings that trap the heat better than blankets. When we got to the passage about Manu Lopez, a sixteen-year-old Luiselli interviewed for his asylum petition, Peter noted that it was Trump who had in fact gone after the Barrio 18 gangs in Hempstead, Long Island. Manu is being questioned about whether or not he has ever been part of a gang on the questionnaire, and he says no, but he didn't feel that much safer in Hempstead than he had in Honduras, which he'd left to escape the gangs. He tells Luiselli, "Hempstead is a shit-hole full of pandilleros, just like Tegucigalpa." I try to navigate what I believe Luiselli is trying to achieve, how the structure of the intake questionnaire helps her organize and shape content. "Americans like to criticize everything," Zeina adds, and the class laughs, though Peter seems more subdued. Isn't this what it means to bang up against blind spots?

What is obvious is obvious—our different backgrounds, cultures, faiths; what isn't is my assumption that what I consider "obvious injustices" are not obvious in the same way to everyone, and not because anyone has any problem seeing and understanding an injustice.

My students see a kind of American naivety at best, at worst perhaps a sense of entitled anger particular to Western sensibilities. I can teach a text which depicts something clearly problematic and inhumane, which to them is more about a collective failure that individual acts of righteousness are unlikely to change. I try to discuss the language of the questionnaire as deliberately out of sync with the realities of the children, as making any chance at a fair assessment of their hopes for asylum unlikely. Again, the majority of my students seem unsurprised and somewhat intrigued by my investment in their views. Here, too, language is what I have—or all I have—and here, too, while we all understand the words and phrases and even the contexts, we are approaching these realities from disparate worlds.

I had listened to Fred Moten, an American cultural theorist, scholar, and poet, who explores Black studies and performance studies, being asked about what was happening in Gaza. He spoke too of how he felt as an NYU faculty member and how "every class should be an experiment in anti-colonization," saying that the challenge for him was to "move beyond the limits of the rhetorical" when tackling difficult subjects. For me those limits had as much to do with the text at hand as my physical and emotional response. My students were repositioning, or deconstructing, how I had constructed my interpretations, and it was uncomfortable.

Versions of the critique that "Americans complain a lot" came up in further discussions, to which I would explain that American culture is built around a notion of self-betterment and progress, an ideal meant to serve all Americans. I explained Luiselli's tone of exasperation, and rage, as in keeping with her subject of migrant children and their vulnerability. "The children are treated more like carriers of diseases than children," she notes, and provides the example that the American Immigration Lawyers Association (AILA) filed a complaint regarding the fact that children in a Dilley, Texas, detention center were given adult-strength hepatitis A vaccines that resulted in their being hospitalized. What I didn't understand was that my response was expressive of a particular worldview, and I had not made enough room in my teaching for the fact that this may not have been a worldview my students shared.

"What are some things you care about in your culture?" I asked Seleem, a Palestinian from Jordan, who said she liked "the limits that tradition gives" and explained she felt comforted by what she called "limits." When I ask for an example, she says that avoiding eye contact with men was one example. Seleem, who wore jeans and kept her long hair uncovered, surprised me with her remark. I'd presumed that she would have wanted the kinds of freedoms Western women had. I offered that in Western cultures making eye contact was often considered a sign of earnestness and sincerity, that looking away could be read as avoidance, even insincerity. "You have to do the work where you are," Moten said, which for him, in that conversation with Jared Ware on *Millennials are Killing Capitalism* (*MAKC*), meant the classroom. I was also in a classroom where we were all using English, but we each seemed to have different interpretations of the words being used. For example, Seleem had no trouble with "limit": it expressed a parameter that provided context and meaning, a cultural signifier she respected.

Limits were also what Luiselli is discussing in an entirely different context, as in what limited the undocumented migrant children's chances for asylum given the language of the intake questionnaire and the window of time available to find a lawyer and make a claim; in 2014, the creation of the "priority juvenile docket" by the Obama administration reduced that window from twelve months to twenty-one days before children would be deported.

If I was attempting to convey a sense of urgency regarding the plight of the undocumented children, I was, like Luiselli, assuming the crisis could be handled differently, that the workings of the state promise to represent not just the rights of its citizens, but humane and humanitarian values upheld in the rhetoric of a North American ideology. "We the People" suggests a body that demands and assumes representation as much as it aims to shape its governing bodies. When Fred Moten spoke of a need "to move beyond the limits of the rhetorical," I think he was suggesting that dominant values come to us packaged in language that can make it difficult to unpack the double standards that contribute to our oppressions.

Luiselli notes that after the unaccompanied child migrant crisis was declared in the United States, and after a meeting between President Barack Obama and Mexico's President Enrique Peña Nieto, Programa Frontera Sur was introduced "to halt the immigration of Central Americans through Mexico." Luiselli points out that the rhetoric is deliberately couched in good intention as "the Mexican government maintains that Mexico must protect the 'safety and rights' of migrants." In fact, the program further compromised the vulnerability of migrants. As "drones; security cameras and control centers in strategic locations (trains, tunnels, bridges . . .)" allowed for "security teams and geolocation technology", the measures amounted to a surveillance mechanism which rewarded the hunt on migrants by vigilantly targeting them. Since 2014, when the program was launched, "Mexico has massively deported Central American migrants, many of whom would have had the legal right to request asylum in either Mexico or the United States". This is to say that while language is there to clarify, or expedite, it also disguises; the factuality of events is glossed over when being apparently addressed in good faith.

What happens when the factuality of events dismantles the rhetorical frames Moten spoke of? Isn't this what Moten means when he says, "You have to do the work where you are"? The concrete differences of "where one is" are collapsed in the spaces of our online world, yet when I see footage of the dead bodies in Gaza, and hear the screams and wailing, a factuality intrudes on how I read these events. A December 24, 2024 news headline reads: "Biden urges caution as Israeli airstrikes kill dozens in one of the war's deadliest nights, Gaza officials say." Biden's use of the word "caution" nearly makes me laugh in disgust but for the grim realization that, not unlike the language in Programa Frontera Sur, this too is an example of rhetorical failure: words like "caution," "safety," or "protection" connote realities that contradict the factuality of events. We enter the ways these words rupture and pervert our assumptions of what "caution" and "safety" mean: there is no caution in how the current Israeli government is decimating Gaza, just as there was no safety or protection for migrants in the Programa Frontera Sur.

In the classroom, I am in a threshold space where the reality of the texts, my reality, and the myriad realities of my students converge. When Russia invaded Ukraine, I put poems by various Ukrainian authors on the course portal for my creative writing class—poems by Lyuba Yakimchuk from her collection *Apricots in Donbas* and work by Victoria Amelina, who was killed at thirty-seven in Kramatorsk when a Russian missile strike hit a restaurant. I had hoped my students would be moved by the words and images, and also the circumstance, but I sensed a detachment. Lines from "my grandmother's fairytale" did not get much reaction as I read: "when tears / turn to rock salt / when the sea in the stomach / turns into a coal mine." Perhaps the images were unfamiliar, references to coal and fruit not part of the Middle

Eastern and African literary landscape, or perhaps these sensations and emotions were already too familiar.

Instead, one of the pieces of writing I received in the class described an exchange with a father who was admonishing his son in the story not to take pleasure in another people's suffering: "Habibi, war is bad anywhere," was the Syrian father's response to the son's remark that "now they know what we went through," a reference to the coverage of war in Ukraine.

I have adjusted the reading lists in my classes several times to better reflect my students' interests and culture, but I want them to experience what I am also experiencing, which is another way of seeing my own cultural positioning, or becoming more conscious of it. Yet I don't always realize that their cultural positioning is already at a slant, in the shadow of empires and geopolitical upheavals. I'll never forget an exchange with Fatima when she told me she would be absent, going home and staying beyond the weekend. "I know it's not London," she said when she mentioned home was Basra, Iraq, to which I laughed, surprised, and said, "Who says London is a preferred destination?" to which she laughed, and added, "The weather's better in Basra. It's very green."

While teaching Khaled Hosseini's *The Kite Runner*, there were several discussions about the differences between the Sunni and Shi'a Muslims—the Shi'as as descendants of the prophet Mohammad's bloodline, the Sunnis as followers of the prophet's way of life, or "Sunna"—who have had their historical conflicts and divides. The novel's focus is on the relationship between Amir, an Afghan Sunni Muslim, and Hassan, a Hazara Shi'a Muslim, his servant and (unbeknownst to Amir until the book's conclusion) his half-brother. What becomes clear in Hosseini's novel is how the social overlay of class and religious difference is secondary to the bonds forged out of love and loyalty as both are contested in the book's various dramas. Rather stunningly, the novel is banned in certain states and schools in the US, where freedom of speech are cultural ideals. While here in the UAE, which does not advertise itself as a democracy and is in fact a monarchy and coalition of regional Sheikhdoms that formed a nation state, I was teaching a book banned in various American schools.

There's a scene in which Hassan is raped by Assef, a German Afghan who spouts racist diatribes about the purity of the Pashtun Afghans whose blood has been compromised by the likes of Hassan's Hazara ethnicity. The irony is that Assef is himself of mixed ethnicities. The students are shocked, and I am a little uncertain about how to discuss this. One student says, "These things happen, we need to know that." The world, we conclude, is in trouble for the fact that notions of purity and a perverse privileging of ethnic origins have overshadowed more fundamental connections among people. Dionne Brand seems to be suggesting this when she says, "Too much has been made of origins," pointing out that while they can be nurturing, they are also arbitrary and indifferent; an excuse for "exclusionary power structures".

My mind is back in Gaza, listening to updates. The fact that the visual images speak a very different story from the updates by the US and Israel shocks me. What happens to language when an event—the bombing of Al Shifa hospital, the Indonesian hospital, the Al-Quds hospital, the Jabalia and Bureij refugee camps—tell another story from Antony Blinken's statement on January 11, 2024: "We are letting more humanitarian aid in for the people who need it." Who is he talking to? In a December 23 *Washington Post* article, "U.N. Security Council Inches Closer to Agreement on Gaza Resolution Vote," the National Security spokesperson John Kirby told reporters who asked why more aid wasn't going into the Gaza Strip. "You have to remember this is a war zone. It's an area of conflict, and that greatly increases the complexity of humanitarian assistance." Indeed. But isn't that the point of "humanitarian assistance"?

Meanwhile, Israel has stalled trucks at entry points and prevented the very basics, such as fuel and water, from reaching the Strip. It seems we have not only failed to articulate the reality—at least in the mainstream media—but we are creating a narrative very different from the reality we are seeing, one that distances and whitewashes the horror. This is the fault line of any officious language: as there is little nuance, one must, in the words of the poet Eleni Sikelianos, work "in the felt space [of] what's not said in the document."

The felt spaces include the stories of children like Dina Abu Mohsen, a twelve-year-old whose leg had been amputated because of the wounds incurred in an Israeli airstrike. The sole survivor of a shelling that killed her parents and two siblings, Dina said that, despite her amputation, she hoped to become a doctor one day to give courage to others like herself. Dina was killed in her hospital bed in the Nasser Medical Hospital in Khan Younis when it was bombed on December 14. Khan

Younis, some nine kilometers from the Rafah border, was supposed to be a safe zone. Hospitals are supposed to be safe zones. There were no safe zones.

There are so many "felt spaces" where we enter shattered. For the victims of war, it is literal. Events can defy language—how to reframe, reconfigure, remake, this reality? The young Palestinian poet Mosab Abu Toha, who managed to leave Gaza through the Rafah border with his young family after having been kidnapped by the IDF, writes in his poem "Palestine A-Z": "'Am' is the linking verb that follows 'I' in the present tense when I am no longer present, when I am shattered." When we are no longer present, words will carry us.

As Valeria Luiselli concludes, she returns to the impasse of language, noting that those minors who cross at the Mexican–American border are not "immigrants" or "illegals" but war refugees, and as such have a right to asylum the existing legal system makes almost impossible to achieve. Her daughter asks, "Tell me what happens next?" And Luiselli answers, "Sometimes I make up an ending, a happy one. But most of the time I just say: I don't know how it ends yet."

Maybe like all endings, this one will teach us how to begin.

REFERENCES

Of event

Kazkaz, Rena. "Mare Nostrum." https://www.imdb.com/title/tt5811176/

Cable, Robert. "Remembering Eleni Bastéa." https://shc.stanford.edu/news/stories/remembering-eleni-bast%C3%A9a

The Journey Where

Beaumont, Peter. "Violence spreads across Israel after shooting in Galilee." *The Guardian*, 9 November 2014. http://mondoweiss.net/2014/11/palestinian-citizens-following#sthash.O1BK75Wz.dpuf

Burgis, Tom, Monieb, Lobna, and Politi, James. "Threat of watery grave rises sharply." *FT Weekend*, 1-2 November 2014.

HSBC brand campaign. "In the Future." www.hsbc.com. http://www.hsbc.com/about-hsbc/advertising/in-the-future

Khatchadourian, Raffi. "We Know How You Feel." *The New Yorker*, 19 January 2014.

Lacey, Hester. "The Inventory: Ann Miura-Ko." *FT Magazine*, 1 November 2014.

Phillips, Adam. *On Kissing, Tickling, and Being Bored*. Cambridge: Harvard University Press, 1993.

Stewart, Susan. *The Poet's Freedom, A Notebook on Making*. Chicago: University of Chicago Press, 2011.

Travis, Alan. "UK axes support for Mediterranean migrant rescue operation." *The Guardian*, 27 October 2014.

The Unhoused

Agamben, Girgio. "Beyond Human Rights." Open 2008/No.15 *Social Engineering*. http://novact.org/wp-content/uploads/2012/09/Beyond-Human-Rights-by-Giorgio-Agamben.pdf

Arendt, Hannah. "We Refugees." *Altogether Elsewhere, Writers on Exile*, ed. Marc Robinson. https://www-leland.stanford.edu/dept/DLCL/files/pdf/hannah_arendt_we_refugees.pdf

Transitional Object, a grammar for letting go

Birkenstein, Cathy. "'As A Result' Connecting the Parts." Gerald Graff, *They Say I Say*. Third edition. W.W. Norton, 2014, pp. 105-20.

Boyer, Anne. "What Is 'Not Writing'?" *Garments against Women*. Boise: Ahsahta, 2015.

Cameron, Daryl, Michael Inzlicht, and William A. Cunningham. "Empathy Is Actually a Choice." *New York Times*. 10 July 2015. Web.

Freud, Sigmund. "The Uncanny." Rpt. in *Web.mit.edu, http://web.mit.edu/allanmc/www/freud1.pdf*

Koestenbaum, Wayne. "Adrienne Rich's Poetry Became Political, but It Remained Rooted in Material Fact." *The New York Times*, 16 July 2016. Web.

Lispector, Clarice. *The Passion According to G.H.* Translated by Idra Novey. New York: New Directions, 2012.

Purpura, Lia. *Bookslut*. http://www.bookslut.com/features/2013_01_019796.php, 2013. Web.

Winnicott, D. W. "Transitional Objects And Transitional Phenomena." *Collected Papers: Through Pediatrics to Psycho-Analysis*. London: International Journal of Psycho-Analysis 34 (1953): 1-34. https://llk.media.mit.edu/courses/readings/Winnicott_ch1.pdf.

The Parts Don't Add Up, an assemblage

Arendt, Hannah. *The Human Condition*. University of Chicago Press, 1958.

Beck, Zeina Hashem. "Naming Things." *3 Arabi Song*, Rattle, 2016.

Bhabha, Homi. "Border Lives: The Art of the Present." https://prelectur.stanford.edu/lecturers/bhabha/location1.html

Benjamin, Walter. "Theses On the Philosophy of History." *Illuminations*. Translated by Harry Zohn. New York: Schocken Books, 1968.

Danish Refugee Council "Closing of borders in Europe is the wrong way to go." News Archive. https://drc.dk/news/news-archive/closing-of-borders-in-europe-is-the-wrong-way-to-go

Shire, Warsan. "Conversations About Home (at the Deportation Centre)." *Teaching My Mother How To Give Birth*. London: mouthmark series, 2011.

~~Left behind~~ for a square of space

Cobb, Allison. *After We All Died*. Boise: Ashanta, 2016.

The *re* in *refuge*

Brand, Dionne. *The Door to the Map of No Return, Notes on Belonging.* New York: Vintage Canada, 2001.

Derrida, Jacques, and Anne Dufourmantelle. *Of Hospitality, Anne Dufourmantelle Invites Jacques Derrida to Respond.* Translated by Rachel Bowlby. Redwood City: Stanford University Press, 2000.

"Psyhi mou"

Adnan, Etel. *Night.* Brooklyn: Nightboat Books, 2016.

Adorno, Theodor W. *Minima Moralia: Reflections from a Damaged Life.* Translated by E.F.N. Jephcott. New York: Verso, 2006.

Bachelard, Gaston. *The Poetics of Space, The Classic Look At How We Experience Intimate Places.* Translated by Maria Jolas. Boston: Beacon Press, 1969.

Cofer, Judith Ortiz. *The Cruel Country.* Athens: University of Georgia Press, 2016.

Ginzburg, Natalia. *The Little Virtues.* Translated by Dick Davis. London: Daunt Books, 2018.

Grill, Genese. "Portals: Cabinets of Curiosity, Reliquaries and Colonialism." *The Missouri Review* 39, no. 1 (2016): 38-62.

Hyde, Lewis. *The Gift, Imagination and the Erotic Life of Property.* New York: Vintage Books, 1983.

Mauss, Marcel. *The Gift: Forms and Functions of Exchange in Archaic Societies.* 1954. Translated by Ian Cunnison. New York: Cohen & West, 1966.

Perec, Georges. *Species of Spaces and Other Pieces.* Edited and translated by John Sturrock. London: Penguin Books, 1997.

The Wig & The Scream, a forensic

Kristeva, Julia. *The Powers of Horror, an essay on abjection.* Translated by Leon S. Roudiez. New York: Columbia University Press, 1982, https://users.clas.ufl.edu/burt/touchyfeelingsmaliciousobjects/Kristevapowersofhorrorabjection.pdf.

Mathews, Aria. *Simulacra.* New Haven: Yale University Press, 2017.

"The Killing" (TV Series 2011-2014), developed by Veena Sud based on the Danish series *Forbrydelsen* ("The Crime") by Søren Sveistrup. https://www.imdb.com/title/tt1637727/

Magnolias

Beck, Koa. "The Legend of Vera Nabokov: Why Writers Pine for a Do-It-All-Spouse." *The Atlantic*, 8 April 2014.

Briante, Susan. *Defacing the Monument*. Blacksburg. Noemi Press, 2020.

Capello, Mary. *Lecture*. San Francisco: Transit Books, 2020.

Didion, Joan. "On Keeping a Notebook." *Slouching Towards Bethlehem*. New York: FSG, 1968.

Lialios, Giorgos. "The 'Great Walk of Athens': Plan to Revamp City Center Unveiled." *Greece is Athens*, 13 May 2020. https://www.greece-is.com/the-great-walk-of-athens-the-plan-to-overhaul-the-city-center/

Nash, Elle. "Dead to Me." *The Adroit Journal*, Issue 35. https://theadroitjournal.org/issue-thirty-five/elle-nash-prose/

Rose, Samantha Hill. "Where Loneliness Can Lead." *Aeon*, 16 October 2020. https://aeon.co/essays/for-hannah-arendt-totalitarianism-is-rooted-in-loneliness

Thurlow, Crispin. "Fakebook: Synthetic media, pseudo-sociality and the rhetorics of web 2.0." January 2013. https://www.researchgate.net/publication/285906889_Fakebook_Synthetic_media_pseudo-sociality_and_the_rhetorics_of_web_20

Tokarczuk, Olga. "The Tender Narrator." The Nobel Prize in Literature, 7 December 2019. www.nobelprize.org/prizes/literature/2018/tokarczuk/104871-lecture-english/

Vassilopoulos, John. "Greek government passes draconian anti-protest legislation." *World Socialist Web Site, WSWS*, 13 July 2020. https://www.wsws.org/en/articles/2020/07/13/gree-j13.html

Borders & belongings

Al-Kateab, Waad and Edward Watts. "For Sama." 2019. https://www.imdb.com/title/tt9617456/

Athens Centre, "Epiphany in Greece." https://athenscentre.gr/epiphany-in-greece/

Derrida, Jacques, and Anne Dufourmantelle. *Anne Dufourmantelle Invites Jacques Derrida to Respond*. Translated by Rachel Bowlby. Redwood City: Stanford University Press, 2000.

Gessen, Masha. "The Russians Fleeing Putin's Wartime Crackdown." *The New Yorker*. March 20. https://www.newyorker.com/magazine/2022/03/28/the-russians-fleeing-putins-wartime-crackdown

Kalfopoulou, Adrianne. "Water." https://partisanhotel.co.uk/Adrianne-Kalfopoulou

Kapllani, Gazmend. *A Short Border Handbook*. London: Granta UK, 2011.

re-

Ilya Kaminsky. "In Occupied Cities, Time Does Not Exist: Conversations with Bucha Writers." *The Paris Review*. June 24, 2022. https://www.theparisreview.org/blog/2022/06/14/in-occupied-cities-time-doesnt-exist-conversations-with-bucha-writers/?fbclid=IwAR3v36YqjG7hoZg6nzhRPUmNhxA9qlIoeakmmOQTsy2Bb5hdhU9C4L7Z888

Erasure timeline

Vorozhbit, Natal'ya. "'I grabbed two rings, took my mother, daughter and the cat': the playwright who fled Kyiv" *The Guardian*. 30 March 2022. https://www.theguardian.com/stage/2022/mar/30/natalya-vorozhbit-diary-of-a-playwright-fleeing-ukraine-bad-roads

Tell me how it ends

Blinken, Antony. @SecBlinken "I met with Egyptian President El Sisi in Cairo to discuss joint efforts to accelerate life-saving humanitarian assistance into Gaza." 11 January 2024. https://twitter.com/SecBlinken/status/1745456484019023918

Brand, Dionne. *The Door to the Map of No Return, Notes on Belonging*. New York: Vintage Canada, 2001.

Luiselli, Valeria. *Tell Me How It Ends, An Essay in Forty Questions*. Minneapolis: Coffee House Press, 2017.

Moten, Fred. "Fred Moten on Palestine and the Nation-State of Israel." With Jared Ware, host of Millennials are Killing Capitalism (MAKC): https://www.bakonline.org/prospections/fred-moten-on-palestine-and-the-nation-state-of-israel/ October, 2023.

Sikelianos, Eleni. "Power of the Pen: Identities and Social Issues in Poetry and Plays. Week 4 Part II: Eleni Sikelianos." https://www.youtube.com/watch?v=PjPDzgKXcAY 2017.

Toha Abu, Mosab. *Things You May Find Hidden in My Ear*. San Francisco: City Lights Books, 2022.

Yakimchuk, Lyuba. *Apricots in Donbas*. Translated by Oksana Maksymchuk, Max Rosochinsky, and Svetlana Lavochkina. Liberty Lake: Lost Horse Press, 2021.

BIOGRAPHICAL NOTE

Adrianne Kalfopoulou is the author of three poetry collections, most recently *A History of Too Much*, and three prose collections including *On the Gaze: Dubai and Its New Cosmopolitanisms*. Her work has appeared in journals, chapbooks and anthologies including *The Harvard Review* online, *World Literature Today*, *Slag Glass City*, *Hotel Amerika*, *Dancing Girl Press* and *Futures: Poetry of the Greek Crisis*. A collection of poems, Ξένη, Ξένο, Ξενιτιά, was translated into Greek with Katerina Iliopoulou. She lives in Athens, Greece.